PRIMO LEVI'S UNIVERSE

A WRITER'S JOURNEY

SAM MAGAVERN

Foreword by Jonathan Rosen

Afterword by Risa Sodi

palgrave
macmillan

PRIMO LEVI'S UNIVERSE
Copyright © Sam Magavern, 2009.

First published in 2009 by
PALGRAVE MACMILLAN®
in the United States—a division of St. Martin's Press LLC,
175 Fifth Avenue, New York, NY 10010.

Where this book is distributed in the UK, Europe and the rest of the
world, this is by Palgrave Macmillan, a division of Macmillan Publishers
Limited, registered in England, company number 785998, of Houndmills,
Basingstoke, Hampshire RG21 6XS.

Palgrave Macmillan is the global academic imprint of the above companies
and has companies and representatives throughout the world.

Palgrave® and Macmillan® are registered trademarks in the United States,
the United Kingdom, Europe and other countries.

ISBN: 978–0–230–60647–0

Library of Congress Cataloging-in-Publication Data

Magavern, Sam.
    Primo Levi's Universe : A Writer's Journey / Sam Magavern.
        p. cm.
    ISBN 978–0–230–60647–0
        1. Levi, Primo—Criticism and interpretation. I. Title.

PQ4872.E8Z7256 2009
853'.914—dc22   2008043353

A catalogue record of the book is available from the British Library.

Design by Newgen Imaging Systems (P) Ltd., Chennai, India.

First edition: July 2009

10 9 8 7 6 5 4 3 2 1

Printed in the United States of America.

CONTENTS

To Monica, my parents, and Carol.

FOREWORD

I N 1987, PRIMO Levi plunged headlong into the stairwell of the apartment building in Turin where he had been born and to which he had returned after his liberation from Auschwitz. Although at the time there was a good deal of debate about the nature and meaning of his death—accident or suicide; illness or cosmic despair—it is surely the way he lived and wrote in the 42 years since the war's end that matter most. If the ancient Greek notion were true that it is the manner of one's death, as much as the substance of one's life, that determines its ultimate meaning, then much of European Jewry, not to mention European civilization, would need to be written off as an abject failure.

Levi is justly revered for his masterful memoirs, beginning with *Survival in Auschwitz*, through *The Reawakening*, *The Periodic Table*, and finally—and most darkly—*The Drowned and the Saved*. *Survival in Auschwitz* was written in a white heat soon after Levi's liberation and was published in 1947, though recognition and translation into other languages came much more slowly. It is often pointed out, but worth repeating, that the American title represents an unfortunate decision by the publisher to replace the haunting Italian title, *Si questo e un uomo*—literally, "If This Is a Man"—with a utilitarian one.

The decision signals a confusion that exists in Levi's reputation and that perhaps existed even within him: the urge to poeticize and philosophize competing at times with the need to bear witness, to record in as literal and straightforward a manner as possible the Nazi war against Western civilization in general and Jews in particular. But in all his work, Levi managed to combine scientific detachment with deep, sympathetic imagination, a combination that allowed him to parse with excruciating clarity all the degradations, large and small, physical and emotional, psychic and spiritual, of the Nazi genocide.

But it allowed him to do much more than that. Sam Magavern's radical interpretation—which happens to be the most sensitive, elegant, and deeply felt portrait of Levi I have read—is that all of Levi's works constitute a great literary epic that traces the evolution of a soul—Levi's own—and represents a coherent portrait of the world—not a small and terrible fragment of the world we visit when we wish to meditate on the darkness of "history," but the world itself.

To be sure, there are complexity and confusion in being a philosopher-witness. And Levi was not merely that; he was also a poet and fiction writer. Though he wrote an honorable novel about a band of Jewish partisans, *If Not Now, When?*, that attempted to combine history and invention (Levi himself was an Italian partisan before his arrest and shipment to Auschwitz), his most successful fictional medium was the short story. He was a master of a peculiar hybrid form, a sort of science fiction that seems half Ray Bradbury and half Franz Kafka parable, with an added undertow of Holocaust awareness that continually threatens to drag the reader into an abyss of dark knowledge, even though the Holocaust and its aftermath are almost never overtly mentioned.

Levi's stories, although they may seem the least consequential aspect of his writing, are a good place to find, in the space of just a few pages, the strange and disconcerting elements of his art. In a deadpan science-fiction story called "Gladiators," recently published in English in the collection *A Tranquil Star*, staged battles between cars and people are all the rage, a sort of modern-day bullfighting. A reluctant man brings his eager girlfriend, but the spectacle sickens both of them. The crowd chants not for death but for mercy when one of the gladiators is wounded, and yet these touches of compassion somehow make the ordeal not only more plausible, but also more painful.

What Levi's story captures, and passes on to the reader, is the guilt that observers feel just for having been there at all; they are implicated by their mere presence. It is the sensation he noticed in the eyes of his Russian liberators in *The Reawakening*, the shame "the just man experiences at another man's crime."

This shame is an indictment of human beings just for being in the midst of a cruel world. For Levi, it was this human stain—as much as the Germans' crimes—that darkened and spread over his long career. His radical humanism kept him from taking refuge in "us and them" distinctions—he was more focused on the shame of the species. (Unlike Elie Wiesel, Levi—a highly assimilated Jew—never quarrels with God, in whom he did not believe even as a young man.)

And yet, simultaneously, the sense of shame implies some inner knowledge of what is indeed right and moral. The exposure of this shame is also, for Levi, a moral pursuit, the cold-eyed breakdown of the complex components that make human beings what they are. Saul Bellow, a great admirer of Levi's, once answered a question about his own need to keep writing novels by recalling an assignment in chemistry class when he was young. Each student was given a black lump of fused elements and told to isolate the constituent parts. Bellow, likening himself to the lump, told the interviewer he still hadn't finished the assignment.

What was for Bellow a playful metaphor was for Levi something far more scientifically serious. A chemist not merely by profession but by temperament and philosophy, Levi really can be considered a scientist-artist. This makes him prophetic of the sort of writer called for by the great biologist Edward Wilson in *Consilience*, a 1998 book suggesting that all knowledge is governed by a handful of laws, that "[n]either science nor the arts can be complete without combining their separate strengths. Science needs the intuition and metaphorical power of the arts, and the arts need the fresh blood of science." Wilson seems to anticipate grand new godless sagas spun out of evolutionary knowledge that will perhaps replace works like the Bible, whose relevance has waned in a rationalist world. Levi, in Magavern's view, is attempting something like this, but with a keen sense of humor, irony, and humility. It is unsurprising that Oliver Sachs, who likewise fills an anomalous literary place as a neurologist-writer, looked to Levi's extraordinary memoir

The Periodic Table, with its organization of episodes built around chemical elements, as an inspiration for his own memoir, *Uncle Tungsten*.

Yet despite Levi's rational stance, human guilt often took on mystical overtones in his work and can seem a sort of belated original sin. It's bound up with the question, which troubles all his writing, of whether his time in Auschwitz was merely a season in hell or a glimpse of the true condition of the world.

Magavern details beautifully the role that Dante played in Levi's thinking, and recounts the episode from "If This Is a Man" in which Levi teaches a fellow prisoner, who does not even understand Italian, verses from *The Inferno*. Recalling the lines, reciting them and passing them on almost literally aid in Levi's survival. Levi's attachment to Dante is not just a story of literary salvation. It raises complex religious questions, not merely by shedding light on how an assimilated Jew recalling an Italian Catholic poet survived a German-built hell. It also sheds a certain theological light on Levi himself. T. S. Eliot wrote that to read Dante is to become, in some sense, Catholic; and although Levi maintained the stance of the skeptical scientist, something of Dante's dark Catholicism—his strong sense of original sin—seems to have seeped into Levi's soul, making the world, even before the Holocaust, appear tainted.

Again it is useful to look at one of Levi's short stories to get a glimpse of his vision of the possibility of transcendent evil. "The Molecule's Defiance," a story collected in English posthumously in *A Tranquil Star*, is a seemingly straightforward account of a night at a paint factory that grows sinister when a vast batch of varnish forms a single monster-molecule and bursts free of its container: "The hatch rose by itself, not suddenly but gently, solemnly, as when tombs open and the dead arise." In the story, palpable dread comes not from the fear of an explosion, the loss of a night's work, or the expectation of reprimand that dogs the chemist on duty, but from a kind of moral sickness, a sense that evil has sunk into the very molecular structure of the world.

In *The Periodic Table*, Levi had offered to the dead of Auschwitz not a spiritual afterlife but a sort of chemical one, imagining, in his final chapter, "Carbon," the way a single atom of carbon might cycle back into the living world, ingested by the author and transformed almost mystically, and yet scientifically, into a dot on the page of the book he is writing.

But this image of rational scientific rescue is undone in a story like "The Molecule's Defiance," where the laws of science do not seem rational at all. Instead of each molecule having "two hands" that form an elegant "rosary," it develops a third hand, and then "every rosary joins with two or three other rosaries, and in the end they've formed a single monster molecule...." Religious imagery overwhelms scientific language, and all the irrational elements from which Levi recoiled in human society seem to have been absorbed into the very fabric of the universe.

But Levi worked against all this, or perhaps it is truer to say that the war between possibilities is given expression in his work, almost as if a Talmudic principle of point and counterpoint, a remnant of his attenuated Jewish past, informed him at a layer even deeper than Dante. He balances philosophical possibilities even as he balances the personal and the historical.

Levi acknowledges the way his human discomfort preceded his enslavement. In *If This is a Man* he identified himself as a repressed young man who, in part because of the
self-consciousness imposed by four years of Italy's Racial
Laws, as well as by temperament, lived before Auschwitz in
"an unrealistic world of my own, a world inhabited by civilized Cartesian phantoms, by sincere male and bloodless
female friendships." Levi was a writer fascinated by repression. He was "liberated" by Auschwitz in certain complex,
paradoxical ways that filled him with both pride and self-
recrimination.

In some sense Levi's endless theme is Freud's theory, in
Civilization and Its Discontents, that man can stand neither
repression nor the lifting of repression. Lacking a divine ideal
of human nature, Levi was constantly exploring the fault lines
of secular humanism—he defended human dignity even as he
developed a growing sense that the human animal was somehow indefensible. Despite many memoirs, he almost never
wrote from the position of husband or father, though he was
both, which further complicates our understanding of his
vision of life. He has become a sort of secular saint, but he
can often seem like Michelangelo's Christ in *The Last Judgment*,
turning away in disgust from the saved even as he consigns the
sinners to hell.

But Levi's heroism as a writer is felt everywhere in his work.
The committed intelligence of his voice offers its own deep
consolation, however bleak his vision became and however
tempted he was to flee, like Gulliver, from a species that had
fallen lower than the beasts. Gulliver began looking at his face
in the mirror as a way of training himself to tolerate the sight

of a human creature again. Levi, in all his writing, held up a mirror to his own mind, and in so doing performed a lasting service. After the barbarisms of the last century—which have followed us into this one—reading Levi remains an indispensable way of readapting ourselves to the human.

Jonathan Rosen
New York, October 2008

CHRONOLOGY OF PRIMO LEVI'S LIFE

1947 Works as an independent chemist with Alberto Salmoni; marries Lucia; publishes *If This Is a Man*.

1948 Begins work at SIVA factory. Birth of first child, Lisa Lorenza.

1953 Promoted to technical director at SIVA.

1957 Birth of second child, Renzo Cesare.

1958 Einaudi publishes edited and expanded *If This Is a Man*.

1961 *If This Is a Man* published in Germany.

1963 *The Truce* is published (U.S. title: *The Reawakening*).

1966 *Storie naturali* (Natural Histories). Some of these stories were later published in English in *The Sixth Day*.

1971 *Vizio di forma* (Structural Defect). Some of these stories were later published in English in *The Sixth Day*.

1975 *The Periodic Table* and Levi's first poetry collection, *L'osteria di Bremen* (The Bremen Beer-Hall) are published.

1977 Full retirement from SIVA factory.

1978 *The Monkey's Wrench* and *Lilìt e altri racconti* (Lilith and Other Stories) are published. Some of the "Lilith" stories were later published in English as *Moments of Reprieve*.

1981 *The Search for Roots* is published.

1984 *If Not Now, When?* and second poetry collection, *Ad ora incerta* (At an Uncertain Hour) are published.

1985 *Other People's Trades* is published.

1986   *The Drowned and the Saved* and *Racconti e saggi*
(Stories and Essays) are published. Some of the sto-
ries and essays later appeared in English as
The Mirror Maker.

1987   Levi dies April 11, 1987, in Turin, Italy.

ONE

A NEW COSMOS

P RIMO LEVI COULD be deceptively modest. Despite the fact that he published some twenty books, in just about every literary genre, he sometimes cultivated the image of a nonliterary author, a *scrittore non scrittore*, as he once phrased it: a writer-witness, a writer-scientist, or an accidental writer. He wrote in solitude, unaffiliated with any universities, literary establishments, circles, or movements. He worked for thirty years as a chemist and manager at a paint and varnish factory. His most famous work is nonfiction, and its subject matter—Auschwitz—is so overwhelming that one can miss its literary depth. He wrote in an age that prized the novel, but his two novels, *The Monkey's Wrench* and *If Not Now, When?*, are not among his most important work.

Yet when we read all of Levi's writings together, we find that he has woven a great and terrifying testament, one of the most vital bodies of work in modern literature. We find that his various writings combine to make a bildungsroman rivaling Proust's. A bildungsroman, or "education novel," follows the moral and psychological growth of its main character. In a minor bildungsroman, we watch a character adapt to an adult reality that we, the readers, already know. In a major bildungsroman, like Proust's or Levi's, we watch as the character finds and creates not only a self, but also a cosmos—a new interpretation of the world.

Levi's main character is Primo Levi: a more or less factual version of himself created in a long series of memoirs, stories, essays, poems, and interviews. In Levi's core work, he focuses on his youth: the classic age for the bildungsroman, the age of adventures. Levi's youth included both adventure and tragedy; it did not end until his late twenties, when he returned from the war, married, and began working as an industrial chemist. But, as important as his youth was to him, Levi continued to grow and change—to re-work himself and his cosmos—until his death.

Levi's central concern was what makes—and unmakes—a man. He pondered this insoluble riddle in diverse ways. He studied the biology of Darwin and the psychology of Freud. He looked to myths and legends, spinning variations on Adam and Eve, the Golem, Frankenstein, and other creation tales. He translated anthropological studies by Claude Levi-Strauss and Mary Douglas. Although not a believer, he studied religious texts, placing the book of Job first in his anthology of favorite works, *The Search for Roots*. Most important, though, he sifted through his own experiences: how his humanity was shaped by Auschwitz, his nine-month odyssey returning from the war, his misadventures as a chemist, his chronic depression, and the challenges of ordinary life. As Levi writes in *The Truce*, "everybody's moral universe, suitably interpreted, comes to be identified with the sum of his former experiences, and so represents an abridged form of his biography."[1]

Levi combined a gift for the lyrical, introspective, and autobiographical with an equally potent gift for the scientific, exploratory, and essayistic. One has to look to Michel de Montaigne to find another writer who reports on his life in a way that encompasses so much of the world. Levi had the tragic misfortune to be present at a crucial event in world history, to suffer personally an epochal, radical evil; but he also had the genius to transmute that experience into enduring literature.

In literary style, Levi is sometimes viewed as a traditionalist. And yet Levi's short stories are playful, ultramodern fables comparable to those of Italo Calvino and Jorge Luis Borges. Some of his poems—such as "For Adolf Eichmann"—have a naked ferocity that could scarcely be called traditional. And Levi's central prose works—*If This is a Man*, *The Truce*, *The Periodic Table*, and *The Drowned and the Saved*—are innovative hybrids of many genres, including autobiography, short story, novel, poetry, essay, history, and sociology. Levi viewed himself as a hybrid, someone not identical with himself; he was like the narrator of *The Monkey's Wrench*, who says, "I felt as if I had two souls in my body, and that's too many."[2]

Levi blurred the line between fact and fiction. While all his autobiographical narratives are more or less true, in some he keeps very close to the facts, changing only a name or a minor detail, but in others he takes considerable license. The results can be confusing. Many of his autobiographical essays, published in the United States in *Moments of Reprieve, Other People's Trades, The Mirror Maker, The Periodic Table,* and *A Tranquil Star,* read exactly like the short stories with which they are intermingled. In Italy, *If This Is a Man* is read as a novel about Auschwitz; in the United States, it is published under the title *Survival in Auschwitz* and presented as historical testimony. One might call it a nonfiction novel, but that hardly does justice to its complex and unstable richness.

Levi's style—so lyrical and yet so polyvalent—responded perfectly to his literary and historical context. By the time he began writing, the era of the great realist novel had passed. It no longer seemed appropriate or original to write in the objective vein of the nineteenth-century masters, surveying society as if from a mountaintop. The focus had shifted to a more subjective account of consciousness: the memories, reflections, dreams, and nightmares of single, often isolated, individuals. As a result, modern literature often runs the risk of solipsism, a retreat into private worlds and languages—something Levi strenuously resisted. His challenge was to write about the world and the self, and their fluctuating, mysterious interactions, in a way that avoided false objectivity and yet remained coherent.

This literary challenge corresponds closely to a modern philosophical challenge: how to create a cosmos—a view of the world—that is systematic enough to be useful and yet open and self-critical enough to avoid hardening into dogma. Secular thinkers have struggled to construct a philosophy that does not rely on God and yet resists the temptation to put man (or history, or some other grand force) in God's place. Scientists have crafted a periodic table (in Italian, *il sistema periodico*), which offers a comprehensive system of natural elements. But what table, what tablets, can give us a comprehensive system of humanity? Or, as Levi asks, "would it not be better to acknowledge one's lack of a system?"[3]

If the Ten Commandments are not divinely given, then it falls to individuals or groups to create their own ethics, their own decalogues. Benito Mussolini offered one response: his Fascist Decalogue, which included the commandment that Mussolini was always right.[4] Levi offered his own ethos, but it included the commandment that he, like all sources, must always be doubted. He grappled with the question of whether we can judge good and evil confidently, and even authoritatively, without becoming authoritarian: whether we can create ourselves without dreaming of being supermen, transcending good and evil.

To respond to these literary and philosophical concerns required a modern Dante, a thinker who could combine stunning ambition with profound humility, bold innovation with "the search for roots." It required someone committed to purity, clarity, and the light of reason, yet capable of celebrating impurity, incoherence, and doubt. Perhaps, to be thoroughly convincing, it required someone with the authority of a firsthand participant: someone who had gone to the edge of the world, the edge of humanity, and seen with his own eyes, suffered with his own body and soul, the demolition and painful re-creation of mankind.

TWO

FROGS ON THE MOON

P RIMO MICHELE LEVI was born in 1919 in Turin, a northern Italian city in the mountainous Piedmont region. His father, Cesare, was an engineer with a lust for life: he enjoyed claret, cigars, music, chess, literature, and a long-standing affair with his secretary.[1] Cesare had a troubled family history. His uncle hanged himself, and his father, Michele Levi, leaped to his death from the second story of a house in 1888. After Michele's death, Cesare's mother married a doctor with whom she had been conducting an affair.[2]

Levi's mother, Ester, came from the stable, established Luzzati family of Turin. Upon her marriage, Ester's parents gave her an apartment at 75 Corso Re Umberto, where she would live the rest of her life, and where Levi, too, would live almost all his life. Ester Levi, in contrast to her husband, was prim, proper, organized, and domestic: the queen of her household. She was emotionally reserved, and Levi once told a journalist that he could not remember a single caress or kiss from her.[3]

Levi had one sibling, Anna Maria, who was two years younger, but bigger and stronger than he. Cesare openly preferred Anna Maria to Primo, who was too frail and serious for his taste. The children were very close growing up, thus setting the pattern for Levi's many friendships with more robust, socially confident people. Levi complained that his father had "no aptitude for the career of fatherhood"; he was often gone, and when he was home he tended to play piano, solve chess problems, or read.[4] When he was a teen, Levi said, Cesare advised him to "drink, smoke, go with girls. But I didn't smoke, I didn't drink, I had no girls."[5] Although they shared a love of books, and Levi enjoyed his father's wide-ranging library, they did not communicate much.[6]

Mussolini took power in 1922, when Levi was three, so he grew up entirely under Fascism. Mussolini, however, did not preach anti-Semitism until the late 1930s, when he was currying favor with Hitler, and up to that point roughly one-third of Italy's Jews, along with the vast majority of all Italians, were Fascists.[7] Levi's father was a member of the party, if an unenthusiastic one, and he enrolled Levi in the Fascist youth movement known as the "Children of the Wolf" when he was five, and the "Avangardia" movement when he was fourteen. This show of loyalty was typical: in 1931 Mussolini required all schoolteachers, professors, and students to swear allegiance to Fascism, and almost all complied.

With few exceptions, Levi did not write about his first ten years. He was not much interested in humans until they began to reason for themselves and confront reality on their own.

Even in *The Periodic Table*, which begins with a swirling, fanciful account of his ancestors and ranges through most of his life, Levi says surprisingly little about his early childhood. And while his family relations form an important subtext for his writings, he wrote almost nothing about his father and mother, and only one story about his sister. Even in his fiction, Levi rarely wrote about families and the relationships between parents, children, and siblings.

One of Levi's few writings about his early childhood is "Frogs on the Moon," in which he describes his encounters with nature during summer vacations. In this memoir-story, the young Levi enjoys learning the names of the grasses and flowers and listening to the birds sing; he even finds a leech gliding through the water to be "graceful, as in a dance." On the other hand, the mole-cricket is an "obese, repugnant, and menacing little monster."[8] At the end of the sketch, he sets some pollywogs free, only to watch one get speared by a robin. The robin is then mangled by a kitten, who carries it off into a corner to toy with it.[9] Over the course of the story, nature has changed from something pleasant to something terrible.

Levi explores his feelings about nature and girls in a memoir-story called "Love's Erector Set." On a summer vacation, young Primo, age eleven, falls in love with nine-year-old Lydia, a homely, sickly, not-too-bright girl with little interest in him. For all her shortcomings, however, Lydia has an intimacy with nature that Levi lacks. Her rapport with animals seems magical, almost a divine gift.[10] She reminds him of Circe in the *Odyssey*, which he has just read in school. Already, at age eleven, Levi feels distant from nature and females; and already he compares his experiences to those of Odysseus. Already, in contrast to a brutal boy named Carlo, whom Lydia prefers, Levi struggles to feel like a man.

Sickly and shy, Levi missed many days of school and once spent a whole year being tutored at home. He stood out in his primary-school class as the youngest, shortest, smartest boy, and the only Jew. His classmates, he says, looked at him as if he were a "strange tiny animal."[11] As a teenager, Levi gained an interest in sports but remained small and awkward. He was fascinated with the tougher boys. In the memoir-story "A Long Duel," he describes his classmates as monstrous oafs, impermeable to knowledge.[12] The most intriguing is Guido, with whom he forms a "polemical friendship":

> Guido was a young barbarian with a sculptural body. He was intelligent and ambitious and envied my scholastic successes; I, symmetrically, envied his muscles, his stature, his beauty, and his precocious sexual lusts.[13]

Levi describes the contests he and Guido devise for each other: slapping each other by surprise, running races at an abandoned stadium, and—Guido's final invention—stripping naked in the classroom when the teacher is not looking. The young Levi is far too modest, but Guido manages to strip and stand on his desk while the teacher is showing the class a skeleton; he is "provocative, Dionysiac, and obscene...an ephemeral monument of terrestrial vigor and insolence."[14] Even as a middle-aged man telling the story, Levi still feels competitive, writing that he does not know which of them has won the long-distance race of life.[15]

As his school years went on, Levi became more athletic, taking up track and field, and made friends more sympathetic than Guido. All his life Levi cultivated close friends to whom he was deeply loyal. Often they were people with qualities he lacked. In *The Periodic Table* he describes his friend Enrico, a poor scholar but a good athlete, with dreams that are realistic, not cosmic:

> He did not experience my tormented oscillation between the heaven (of a scholastic or sports success, a new friendship, a rudimentary and fleeting love) and the hell (of a failing grade, a remorse, a brutal revelation of an inferiority which each time seemed eternal, definitive).[16]

But even Enrico, for all his "virile attributes," has been rendered impotent by his upbringing.[17] When he and Levi sneak into the lab of Enrico's older brother to do chemistry experiments, they feel embarrassed by their lack of skill. Unlike their mothers, who know how to sew, cook, play the piano, and paint, the boys, like their fathers, are not handy. Their hands are coarse, yet weak; they can play and write, but cannot use the hammer and blade, which have been "too cautiously forbidden" to them. As a result, they feel deficient: "If man is a maker, we were not men: we knew this and suffered from it."[18]

Levi attributes the boys' sense of physical inadequacy to Jewishness: what he calls an ancient atrophy of family and caste.[19] In an interview with Philip Roth, he elaborates on this theme: "Some 'Aryan' schoolmates jeered at us, saying that circumcision was nothing but castration, and we, at least at an unconscious level, tended to believe it, with the help of our puritanical families."[20] Levi's father, Cesare, the philandering bon vivant, was decidedly not puritanical. It seems to have been his mother whose attitudes he found repressive. But it was not just his mother and the anti-Semites who made Levi feel less than a man. It was also his looks and his personality; even one of his Jewish classmates described him as "a bit of a joke, frankly, something of a prig—his name was a byword for sexual backwardness."[21]

As he was finishing high school in 1936, Levi suffered a major trauma, which he recounts in the story "Fra Diavolo on the Po." He was summoned before the War Ministry and falsely accused of having ignored a draft notice for the navy. Levi was terrified that he would be thrown in jail or sent to sea; he did not even know how to swim. The very next day, he had to write a final exam on the patriotic theme of Italy's entry into the Spanish Civil War vis-à-vis a quote from Thucydides: "We have the singular merit of being brave to the utmost degree." Levi, understandably, was feeling neither patriotic nor brave, and he failed the exam, which meant having to retake all his exams several months later. He describes his failure, the first bad grade he had ever received, as feeling like a death sentence.[22] Although he does not say so explicitly in the story, he appears to have suffered a nervous breakdown; it was, his sister said, a family tragedy.[23]

Luckily, Levi's father was able to keep him out of the navy by signing him up for the Fascist militia. Thus, for his first year of university—until the Racial Laws of 1938 banished Jews from the militia—he went marching every Saturday morning with his troop. Levi comments that at the time he was neither a Fascist nor an anti-Fascist. He never learned to use a gun, the uniform gave him no pride, and the boots chafed his ankles raw, but he did enjoy marching in step to music: "It was a dance, and it gave me the sensation of belonging to a human alliance, of merging with a unified group."[24] Not even this military dance, however, could make Levi feel like a complete man, when he had never danced with a girl.

THREE

BLACK STARS

L EVI ENTERED THE Chemistry Institute at the University of Turin in 1937: a friendly but intense young man with a fierce, almost messianic ambition to understand and master the cosmos for himself. He describes his urgency in *The Periodic Table*:

> [C]hemistry represented an indefinite cloud of future potentialities which enveloped my life to come in black volutes torn by fiery flashes, like those which had hidden Mount Sinai. Like Moses, from that cloud I expected my law, the principle of order in me, around me, and in the world.... I would watch the buds swell in spring, the mica glint in granite, my own hands, and I would say to myself: "I will understand this, too. I will understand everything, but not the way *they* want me to. I will find a shortcut, I will make a lock-pick, I will push open the doors."[1]

Given the type of revelations he sought, it may seem surprising that Levi chose to study chemistry instead of literature, philosophy, or religion. But he came from a family of engineers, and his high school teachers had praised his scientific ability, not his writing skill. He was also reacting against Fascist dogma, which identified the humanities with Spirit and science with vulgar and grubby materialism. Levi found the clarity and verifiability of chemistry a welcome tonic to the Fascists' windy, toxic rhetoric.

Levi had additional reservations about philosophy. When, at the end of his life, an interviewer asked if he distrusted philosophers as he distrusted prophets, Levi answered:

> Well, yes. Perhaps because of ignorance. Listen, I've always made paints, I'm used to a concrete life, in which you either solve a problem or throw it away. Philosophical problems, by contrast, haven't changed since the Pre-Socratics, they keep going around and around them, working them over and over…And also, all philosophers share the vice of wanting to invent their own private language which you need to struggle your way through before you can understand what they mean.[2]

Levi's answer blends modesty and pride. He portrays himself as an ignorant paint-maker, and yet he judges philosophers quite harshly for two flaws: they invent their own languages, and they make no progress. Levi, by contrast, wants an interpretation of reality that is comprehensible to all and reflects the progress scientists like Darwin and Einstein have made in understanding reality.

Nor did religion call out to Levi. The Italian Jews were perhaps the most assimilated Jews in Europe. Levi's family observed the holidays but was essentially secular. "It's as if my religious sense had been amputated," he once told an interviewer. "I just haven't got one."[3] While Levi was at university, he joined some friends in a Jewish study group, formed in response to the passage of the Racial Laws. In *The Periodic Table,* he describes how they gathered in the gym of the Jewish elementary school and tried to find in the Bible the strength to overcome injustice. But this experiment ended in disenchantment: the God who had dictated the Law to Moses "no longer inspired anyone," and the sky above was "silent and empty."[4]

Uninterested in philosophical or religious solutions, Levi turned to chemistry, searching not so much for a profession as for what he called a "vision of the world."[5] His vision was surprisingly aggressive.

> We would dredge the bowels of the mystery with our strength, our talent: we would grab Proteus by the throat, cut short his inconclusive metamorphoses from Plato to Augustine, from Augustine to Thomas, from Thomas to Hegel, from Hegel to Croce. We would force him to speak.[6]

Although he found chemistry more meaningful than religion or philosophy, as he worked his way through university, Levi realized that this violent interrogation of nature was not giving him the fundamental answers he wanted. And so he decided to go back to the origins: to physics.

Levi and a classmate, Sandro Delmastro, began to study physics together, and Levi tried to explain to Sandro his latest dream of conquering matter:

> That the nobility of Man, acquired in a hundred centuries of trial and error, lay in making himself the conqueror of matter... That conquering matter is to understand it, and

understanding matter is necessary to understanding the universe and ourselves: and that therefore Mendeleev's Periodic Table, which just during those weeks we were laboriously trying to unravel, was poetry, loftier and more solemn than all the poetry we had swallowed down in *liceo;* and come to think of it, it even rhymed![7]

In his vision, physics is conquest, but also poetry: it is "the bridge, the missing link, between the world of words and the world of things."[8]

Under the Racial Laws, Levi was not allowed to become a professional physicist. For a time, however, he planned to do it anyway: "I would become a physicist, *ruat coelum:* perhaps without a degree, since Hitler and Mussolini forbade it."[9] *Ruat coelum*—"though the heavens should fall"—is the short form of a Latin maxim, "Let justice be done, though the heavens should fall." The quotation mingles Levi's desire to rebel against Fascism with his desire to shake the foundations of the cosmos itself. After several professors rejected him because he was Jewish, Levi found a young astrophysicist, a teaching assistant named Nicoló Dallaporta, to supervise his experimental thesis.

Physics ended—like philosophy, religion, and chemistry—in disenchantment, although of a different nature. In *The Periodic Table,* Levi tells how Dallaporta punctured his faith in physics as an ultimate revelation, "harpooning" his "last hippogriff."[10] Even physics, Dallaporta said, was marginal: it regulated only appearances, while the essence of things remained hidden behind a veil. Dallaporta sought the essence in a mystical, philosophical Hinduism. But Levi was never tempted by mysticism, and he believed that science did uncover reality, not just appearances. The problem was that the reality it revealed was terrifying, incomplete, and not entirely comprehensible.

Levi felt that modern physics was effecting the most important of all cultural revolutions, surpassing even the radical decenterings inflicted by Copernicus and Darwin.[11] He ends his anthology, *The Search for Roots*, with an essay on black holes entitled "We Are Alone," introducing it with these thoughts:

> Not only are we not in the center of the universe, but the universe is not made for human beings; it is hostile, violent, alien. In the sky there are no Elysian Fields, only matter and light, distorted, compressed, dilated, and rarified to a degree that eludes our senses and our language.[12]

The stars, for Levi, are no longer the familiar symbols with which Dante ended each section of *The Divine Comedy*. They do not transmit messages of peace and poetry, but other messages, "ponderous and disquieting."[13] The old faiths of Homer, Moses, and Dante have been dissolved by science, but a new cosmos has yet to be fashioned. To do so, Levi says, will require a scientist-poet, but even he may fail: "the scientist-poet is not yet born and perhaps never will be born who is able to extract harmony from this obscure tangle, make it compatible, comparable, assimilable to our traditional culture."[14]

Levi, a scientist-poet himself, gives perhaps his most eloquent, desperate summa of our cosmic predicament in his poem "The Black Stars." In it he says that the constellations are now a "tangle of monsters" and the sky is strewn with "horrible dead suns." The black stars do not emit energy, messages, or light: just a desperate heaviness. Echoing Ecclesiastes, but in a still darker key, he concludes that we, like the skies, live and die in vain.[15] If Levi's studies in chemistry and physics at university were exciting and challenging, they were also profoundly disturbing, as he confronted for the first time the black holes that would consume him for the rest of his life.

Academically, the Chemistry Institute was a brutal environment, led by an old despot named Professor Ponzio, whom Levi calls a "savage" and a "hunter."[16] In *The Periodic Table* he describes Ponzio's initiation ritual, in which the students were torn from their books and plunged into a lab filled with "eye-smarting fumes, hand-scorching acids, and practical events that do not jibe with the theories."[17] Ponzio used natural selection, writes Levi, to pick those "most qualified for physical and professional survival."[18] Indeed, only thirty of the initial eighty students graduated. For Levi, the Racial Laws, defining Jews as subhuman and imposing a broad array of burdens, made the environment even rougher and more alienating. But Levi excelled in his studies, and he made several close friends.

His two best friends, Sandro Delmastro and Alberto Salmoni, shared Levi's new passion for mountain climbing, a sport that, ironically, had been popularized by Nietzscheans and Fascists.[19] Roped together on a mountain, Salmoni later recalled, "we were *physically* bound in every sense—a triplet—and it made for a very powerful camaraderie."[20] A female friend remembered this tight trio as "almost misogynist," and for Levi, these male friendships were intense and romantic.[21] Levi devotes the chapter "Iron" in *The Periodic*

Table to his friendship with Sandro. He describes its inception in this unusual passage:

> I had noticed with amazement and delight that something was happening between Sandro and me.... [H]e had an elusive, untamed quality... [N]othing had gotten through his carapace of reserve, nothing of his inner world, which nevertheless one felt was dense and fertile.....He had the nature of a cat with whom one can live for decades without ever being permitted to penetrate its sacred pelt.[22]

Sandro is the man of iron, but Levi describes him in feminine terms—"fertile," a cat whose pelt one can't penetrate. In their symbiosis, Levi provides the abstract mastery and Sandro the practical. Sandro starts reading more, and his grades improve, while he offers Levi a new intimacy with the physical world:

> He proved to me without too much difficulty that I didn't have the proper credentials to talk about matter. What commerce, what intimacy had I had, until then, with Empedocles' four elements? Did I know how to light a stove? Wade across a torrent? Was I familiar with a storm high up in the mountains? The sprouting of seeds? No. So he too had something vital to teach me.[23]

Mountain climbing with Sandro is practical, yet cosmic: Levi calls the rocks and ice of the mountain the true, authentic, timeless *Urstoff* ("element" or "primal substance").[24] When Sandro and Levi get trapped on the high peaks one night, they regard it not as an embarrassing fiasco, but a perverse triumph. They liken it to eating bear meat: it tastes like being the master of one's destiny.[25]

As Levi survived his initiation with Ponzio in the laboratory and his initiations with Sandro and Alberto in the mountains, he felt in some ways that at last he was becoming a man. But socially, he was still struggling, as anti-Semitism isolated him and compounded his natural shyness. In the chapter titled "Zinc" in *The Periodic Table*, Levi writes that, denied a woman's smile, which he needed as much as air, he felt condemned to permanent masculine solitude.[26] Levi softens the desperation by granting his literary self a small victory—the courage to take a girl's arm—that, in real life, he probably did not achieve.[27] In Levi's other writings, the despair and sexual horror are more intense. In "Dialogue of a Poet and a Doctor," he describes a young poet who finds the universe meaningless. Tormented by unrequited love and the sense of his unattractiveness, he wonders, "What was the point of living?"[28] During his university years, Levi himself sometimes doubted the point of living, and he once confided thoughts of suicide to Alberto.[29]

Throughout his life, Levi identified strongly with the great nineteenth-century poet of despair, Giacomo Leopardi: a frail, sickly hunchback consumed by unrequited love. In a draft of Levi's unfinished novel, *The Double Bond*, the narrator says that, as a young man contemplating suicide, he read Leopardi "as perhaps no one else has ever read him, trying to see myself in him, to draw comfort from his despair."[30] Leopardi's family situation may have struck Levi as a nightmarish exaggeration of his own: Leopardi's father was highly irresponsible but maintained a splendid library; his mother was pious but cold and heartless.

In Levi, as in Leopardi, despair includes a complicated tangle of feelings about sex. Levi creates a character in "The Sixth

Day" who says that sex is "a permanent source of dangers and troubles," and that the fact that "orifices and channels meant for excretions" have been used for sexual purposes is a "mocking symbol, an abject and disturbing confusion, the sacred-foul mark of a two-headed unreason, of chaos."[31] Elsewhere, in a seemingly slight essay on spiders, Levi shows his horror of the sexual "Mother Enemy":

> The spider's technique of capture—tying up the prey caught in its web with its silken thread—would make it a symbol of maternity. The spider is the Mother-Enemy who enfolds and engulfs us, who wants to make us re-enter the womb from which we have come; to bind us tightly, so that we return to the impotence of infancy, and she can take us back into her power.[32]

No wonder Levi suffered from arachnophobia as a boy! At the end of this essay, Levi mentions how as a child he "collided" with the Gustave Doré illustration of Arachne for *The Inferno*—how Dante, on his knees before the monster, seems to be "contemplating its crotch, half disgusted, half voyeur."[33]

It is not just spiders, but nature itself that is the Mother-Enemy. Levi once told an interviewer that, in the absence of God, he emulated Leopardi, who accused nature of deceiving her children with false promises of happiness.[34] Levi titled a poem, a story, and a collection of stories "Lilith," after the Jewish embodiment of evil, feminine nature. In medieval folklore, Lilith is Adam's first, demonic wife, who hunts out newborn babies and tries to kill them. In his poem, Levi describes her as beautiful down to her waist, but below that a will-o'-the-wisp.[35] A will-o'-the-wisp is a light that appears in the night over marshy ground, caused by the combustion of gas from decomposed organic matter; it also means a deceptive goal or hope. For Levi, Lilith is the sexualized version of the decomposing organic: she is deceptive Mother Nature, and she is death. In the story "Lilith," Levi recounts a kabbalistic tale of Lilith seducing God himself: a cosmic descent into chaos and evil, which will persist until a (male) messiah comes.

In "Out of the Cradle Endlessly Rocking," Walt Whitman ravels motherhood, sex, death, and nature into a great web—a cosmos—and embraces it, finding in it his poetic vocation. Young Levi, facing a similar web, found himself turned to stone. It was not just that he lacked confidence with women and sexuality; he was also repulsed by them, to the point where he felt unable to feel desire—only a fascinated, appalled torment. As the narrator in *The Double Bond* draft says, "I would shadow them as far as their houses, and then spend hours beneath their lighted windows, trying to interpret the rare shadows I caught sight of, determined to make no move, yet jealous to the point of madness."[36]

Levi related matter, the basic stuff of the cosmos, to what was "the matter" with him: his feelings about his mother, women, and sexuality. Hence, to grow up and become a man, Levi had to conquer mother-matter, which, inevitably, meant a struggle with his self as well as his world. As he told an interviewer:

> Matter is maternal, even etymologically, but it is also inimical....And in any case, man too is matter and is thus in conflict with himself, as all religions have acknowledged. Matter is also an education, a genuine school for life. Fighting against it, you mature and grow.[37]

To be a man meant to be strong and free, the master of one's destiny; but for Levi such freedom could be achieved only by conflict: conquering matter through chemistry and mountaineering, and conquering women through...what? How? Here, Levi was caught in a double bind. He remained frightened of women as romantic partners, and his sense of duty made it impossible for him to separate from his mother. To master meant to understand, but Levi felt blocked from understanding women and his feelings about them.

FOUR

MAGIC MOUNTAINS

I N 1941, LEVI graduated from university *summa cum laude*, scoring 110 out of 110 on his final exam.[1] He was now a brilliant inorganic chemist and an amateur mountaineer blessed with several close friendships. But still he felt incomplete: pained by romantic frustration, the rising tide of anti-Semitism that barred him from becoming an astrophysicist, and his general sense of the world as a blind and hostile chaos. Without a fulfilling love for flora, fauna, or women, he found the world, not surprisingly, a place of rocks and of men who were sometimes friendly but most often were in competition with each other and the flinty, ungiving, mother-matter of the world.

For Levi, life was like mountaineering, and mountaineering meant measuring himself against extremes; it was his version of the struggles depicted by some of his favorite authors: Joseph Conrad, Jack London, and Herman Melville.[2] In *The Periodic*

Table, he writes, "We are chemists, that is hunters: ours are 'the two experiences of adult life' of which Pavese spoke, success and failure, to kill the white whale or wreck the ship."[3] Levi prized his work with matter, unlike the Fascist writers who celebrated only Spirit, and yet he, too, viewed matter as "Spirit's great antagonist," filled with "obtuse and malign inertia."[4]

But if the earth was a rocky mountain, Levi still hoped to climb to its summit and extract riches from its mysterious depths. One of his favorite books at the time was, appropriately enough, Thomas Mann's *The Magic Mountain,* and life, for all its desolate stretches, also offered considerable enchantment. In December 1941, Levi was hired at an asbestos mine to attempt to extract nickel from the slag, a misadventure he recounts in *The Periodic Table.* Despite its bleak ugliness, resembling Dante's representations of hell, the mine was also "magical," with a "wild enchantment."[5] Wandering near it on moonlit nights allowed Levi to forget his troubles: the Nazis were triumphing, and his father was dying of cancer back in Turin. This mingled scene of desolation and magic, freedom and dark fate, inspired him to write his first two short stories, which he included in *The Periodic Table* as "Lead" and "Mercury." In describing how the mountain region gave birth to his stories, Levi writes:

> For that rock without peace I felt a fragile and precarious affection: with it I had contracted a double bond, first in the exploits with Sandro, then here, trying as a chemist to wrest away its treasure. From this rocky love and these asbestos-filled solitudes . . . were born two stories. . . .[6]

Many of Levi's ambiguous feelings about the world are here in microcosm. The world, too, is a "rock without peace" for which he feels a "fragile and precarious affection": a "double bond." In the Italian idiom, "double bond" means both a "double bind"—an impossible dilemma—and the way that organic molecules attach to each other in more than one place, allowing for richer but more unstable combinations.[7] *Double Bond* is also the name of Levi's last, unfinished book, in which he attempts to describe the messy, volatile worlds of organic chemistry, sadness, and love.

Levi's life at the mine was exciting but lonely, and his work proved a failure: it was not feasible to retrieve nickel from the slag. After five months there, he needed to find a new job—no easy thing, given the prohibitions on employing Jews. Luckily, an old classmate, Gabriella Garda, recommended him for a job as a chemist at a laboratory in Crescenzago, near Milan. In June 1942, Levi quit the mine and moved to Milan with a few indispensable possessions, including his editions of Rabelais and *Moby Dick*, and his mountain-climbing equipment.

In Milan, Levi became more culturally and politically aware, living with bohemian friends who wrote poetry and were beginning to resist Fascism. Inspired by his new milieu, he wrote an unpublished fable called "Man"—a direct attempt to understand human nature. In the beginning, Man lives on the edge of nothingness. When he decides to enter the world, he is drawn to the mountains. Then he finds himself sleepless, high on a peak, and thinks about himself. He thinks about "the one true mystery—our existence as thinking beings." But the thought of himself is like an abyss into which he could vanish, and so he "sees that there are limits to understanding" and draws back from the brink.[8] Man is an enigma that he must, but ultimately cannot, fathom.

Meanwhile, Levi was falling in love with Gabriella, who worked with him in the lab at Crescenzago. She was engaged to another man, but she flirted with Levi, riding around town on the handlebars of his bicycle during their lunch breaks. In the chapter titled "Phosphorus" in *The Periodic Table*, Levi describes their time together, but renames her "Giulia." When Levi describes his first encounter with laboratory rabbits, his feelings about Gabriella lurk just below the surface:

> Rabbits are not attractive animals. They are among the mammals most distant from man, perhaps because their qualities are those of humanity when humiliated and outcast: they are timid, silent, and evasive, and all they know is food and sex. Except for some country cat in my distant childhood, I never had touched an animal, and faced with the rabbits I felt a distinct revulsion...[9]

Paradoxically, Levi hates rabbits for being "distant from man," but he describes that distance as a similarity to man when he is downtrodden. In other words, rabbits are distant from our true humanity, our higher selves, but all too close to our lower selves. This passage has echoes in Levi's writings about "humiliated and outcast" Auschwitz prisoners, reduced to beasts. It also resonates with Levi's feelings about Gabriella, whom he describes as a "lioness," but whom he also finds a bit too free and easy, a bit too "rabbitlike," when it comes to love.[10]

Levi wrote cloying verses to Gabriella, which he never published.[11] But by February 1943, after she had married, Levi had purged himself of sentimentality and was ready to write his first fully mature work, a poem called "Crescenzago" about the factory town where they had worked. In the poem, Levi describes how the wind veers away, afraid that the factory's poisoned smoke will rob its breath. The children's faces are the color of dead dust. The women never sing, but trams whistle constantly and raucously. The workers toil all day to keep "the grim black stonecrusher panting."[12] Levi ends the poem with the workers making love on Saturday nights in the ditch by the railroad, conveying both envy and disgust, perhaps a transmuted echo of his frustrations with Gabriella.

What is most striking about "Crescenzago," though, is how closely it resembles "Buna," the first poem Levi wrote after the war. "Buna" is also about dawn in a desolate place of smokestacks, whistles, and colorless, broken people, but it describes the factory at Auschwitz. As important as Auschwitz was to Levi as a writer, his first three stories and, especially, "Crescenzago," demonstrate that he had already found his voice and his basic themes: what makes a man, what contemporary man has done to nature and to himself, and what we can make of a new and desolate universe.

Levi's fundamental quest was to understand, and thus master, the world. He turned to writing, perhaps, because anti-Semitism barred him from being a physicist and because, increasingly, he sought to understand not just the natural world but also humanity, particularly as it collapsed into evil and chaos all around him. One is reminded of a thinker Levi much admired, Sigmund Freud, who also had found his path to more prestigious forms of scientific research barred by anti-Semitism. Partly in response, he had chosen the epigraph for *The Interpretation of Dreams* from Virgil's *Aeneid*: "If I cannot

bend the Higher Powers, I shall move the Infernal Regions."
Levi, denied the chance to study the stars, became the master
chronicler of hell on earth.

In 1943, as the Germans took over northern Italy, Levi and
many of his friends fled to the mountains and joined the resistance. But his partisan days were truncated, terrifying, and
a source of shame, not pride, for him. He and his friends, a
comrade later recalled, were childish—merely playing at being
partisans.[13] Levi writes in *The Periodic Table* that he carried a
revolver that he was not sure how to use; it was "tiny, all inlaid
with mother of pearl, the kind used in movies by ladies desperately intent on committing suicide."[14] Although he played
no direct part in it, Levi was horrified when his partisan group
executed two members for breach of duty. After forty-five days
of confusion, Levi and several of his friends were betrayed and
captured.

After his capture, Levi was interned in an Italian prison
camp at Fossoli. He was with a fellow partisan and chemist
named Vanda Maestro, and they had fallen in love, but their
situation was unbearably tragic. One source suggests that
Vanda wanted to sleep with Levi but he declined, and that, on
the last night before deportation to Auschwitz, she slept with
the Italian commandant in a vain attempt to save her life.[15] The
next morning, she slit her wrists but survived.[16] Levi may be
referring to these events, among others, when he writes in *If
This Is a Man*, "Many things were then said and done among us;
but of these it is better that there remain no memory."[17]

Vanda spent the five days of the awful train ride pressed
in Levi's arms before being torn from him upon arrival at the
camp.[18] She survived the initial selections and lived in the Lager

for eight months before being murdered by the Nazis, as Levi reports with heartbreaking exactitude in *The Truce*: "Vanda had died by gas, fully conscious, in the month of October."[19] What makes this passage so mysterious is that nowhere else in *The Truce* does Levi name Vanda; in reading about her death, the reader has no way of knowing what she meant to Levi.

FIVE

HELL'S CIRCLES

ON FEBRUARY 26, 1944, Levi found himself in Auschwitz: a black hole on earth. He was, in his words, a man stripped of "everyone he loves...his house, his habits, his clothes, in short, of everything he possesses."[1] He was in hell, but Levi found, as Dante had, that hell is an excellent place to study mankind. As his Auschwitz comrade Charles Conreau once wrote, Levi was a "marvelous weigher of souls."[2] Levi weighed and re-weighed the souls of Auschwitz for the rest of his life: in his first book, *If This Is a Man,* in his last, *The Drowned and the Saved*, and in many works in between.

Like Dante, Levi was deeply concerned with justice, but he needed to forge new meanings for the word. As an atheist, he could not rely on divine justice, and traditional concepts of human justice also seemed inadequate to deal with the magnitude of the Nazi offense. It was, for Levi, "an abomination, which no propitiatory prayer, no pardon, no expiation by the guilty, which nothing at all in the power of man can ever clean again."[3] Moreover, it was not just the Nazis' direct crimes that confounded old ideas of justice. In the Lagers, the Nazis created an entire realm in which normal morals no longer functioned, even in the inmates' relations with each other.

The Nazi hell was a total system—like the periodic table or *The Divine Comedy*—but a mad one, filled not with measured punishments but useless violence. As Levi writes in *If This Is a Man*, the prohibitions were innumerable; the rites were infinite and senseless.[4] The prisoners had to make their beds perfectly even though they were forced to live in intolerable filth. They had to shine their wooden clogs, but there was no polish; they used tar, fat, or machine grease purchased on the black market. In Levi's view, in the Lager there were no criminals, because there was no moral law to violate, and no madmen, because the prisoners were devoid of free will.[5]

No received wisdom could make sense of this world. Levi had to sift through his experiences with the utmost care and patience. In doing so, he taught himself the art of judgment. Years later, as an industrial chemist, when he met a new client, he instinctively assessed how that person would have fared at Auschwitz; he said that he could get the measure of a man in a split second.[6] Like Dante, Levi drew fine gradations between people: he carefully measured the circles of hell, not only distinguishing victims from oppressors, but also examining the vices and virtues of the victims.

Although *If This Is a Man* begins with a date ("I was captured by the Fascist Militia on December 13, 1943") and ends with a dated account of ten days (January 18–27, 1945), the middle of the book is not strictly chronological.[7] According to Levi, this timelessness reflects the world of the Lager, where the days all seemed alike, and one quickly learned to wipe out the past and the future.[8] For the prisoners, history had stopped.[9] But Levi—like Dante—also has literary reasons for creating a timeless realm; he wishes to explore the existential parameters of life. Therefore, he does not write a simple chronicle, but a literary work of uncertain genre, using the tools of a memoirist, novelist, short story writer, poet, essayist, historian, and scientist.

Because Levi is interested primarily in Auschwitz as a microcosm, *If This Is a Man* relates almost nothing about life outside the Lager. Levi rarely refers to the course of the war. We learn almost nothing about his family, upbringing, or nation. He makes allusions, but generally to timeless classics: the Bible and *The Inferno*. He rarely discusses the cultures and subcultures that produced his fellow inmates. He is interested in the "demolition of man," not in the demolition of Jewish culture. In later stories, like "Lilith," Levi is willing to serve as a cultural transmitter, repeating a Jewish tale filled with the "unassuageable sadness that grows on the ruins of lost civilizations."[10] But to do so in *If This Is a Man*, he seems to feel, would introduce extraneous elements into the experiment; it would muddy the distillation.

Auschwitz lies at the limits of language. Paradoxically, Levi carefully and authoritatively describes Auschwitz while protesting that words are inadequate. He says that "our language lacks words to express this offence, the demolition of a man."[11] He says that words like "hunger," "tiredness," "fear," "pain," and even "winter" will not suffice, because they are "free words, created and used by free men."[12] He says that if "the Lagers had lasted longer a new, harsh language would have been born," and that only this language could express the inmates' experiences.[13] And yet, by its literary mastery, his book belies its own claims of ineffability. Levi believes that his words reflect Auschwitz truly, but only because they do not pretend to reflect it completely.

Levi wrote about Auschwitz for 42 years, from his homecoming in 1945 until his death in 1987. He wrote about it in poems, memoirs, book reviews, stories, essays, articles, letters, museum plaques, and even in a medical treatise. By returning to the subject over the years and in many genres, Levi was able to express different facets of the experience and even to contradict himself. In "The Gypsy" and "The Gray Zone" he tells us there was no camaraderie in the Lager, but in "Our Seal" he writes that his work squad had a certain esprit de corps, a rough friendship.[14] In *If This Is a Man*, we learn that every prisoner was corrupted; but in "The Disciple," we meet Bandi, who cannot be corrupted by humiliation; rather, he is somehow purified by it.[15] *If This Is a Man* portrays the inmates as incapable of curiosity; but in "The Quiet City," one of the most frequent states of mind is curiosity.[16] These contradictions, far from being flaws, are part of Levi's truthfulness, reflecting the impossibility of a static understanding of the Lager.

Levi rarely repeats himself. *The Drowned and the Saved* shares its title with one of the chapters in *If This Is a Man*, published four decades earlier, yet it is a very different exploration, in both style and content. Levi knows that being a firsthand witness gives him a crucial, but imperfect, perspective. As he writes in *The Drowned and the Saved,* "[f]or knowledge of the Lagers, the Lagers themselves were not always a good observation post: in the inhuman conditions to which they were subjected, the prisoners could barely acquire an overall vision of their universe."[17] Even slight differences in perspective matter because, as Levi notes, two eyewitnesses to the same event almost never describe it the same way.[18] Therefore, he remains open to modifying his views, and even the meaning of his memories:

> ...these memories do not fade, nor do they thin out. They become enriched with details I thought were forgotten, which sometimes acquire meaning in the light of other people's memories, from letters I receive or books I read.[19]

In thinking about Levi's views of Auschwitz, one must shuttle constantly from one work to another and remember that no words are final. A true story, as he reminds us in *Moments of Reprieve,* "is pregnant, asks more questions than it answers, and leaves us in suspense; it cries out and demands to be interpreted."[20]

In the preface to *If This Is a Man,* Levi seems to suggest that he will focus on the humanity, or lack of humanity, of the Nazis.[21] But although he tried all his life to fathom the Nazis, Levi wrote relatively little about them in his first book. One reason was that he knew few of them firsthand. The Lager was administered mostly by the inmates themselves, especially the relatively privileged "green triangles," who were neither Jews nor political prisoners but ordinary German criminals. As a result, there are few memorable evil characters in the book; there is no Satan or Mephistopheles.

The first exemplar of evil is the nameless guard who snatches away the icicle Levi is using to quench his thirst. "Why?" Levi asks. "There is no why here," the guard replies.[22] Evil is an attempt to defeat understanding. There are myriad rules in the camp, but they are senseless. The guards communicate not in words, but in blows, useless violence, the anti-language of brute domination. The paradigmatic evil, for Levi, is to treat someone as less than human, especially by refusing to speak with him.

The two most notable evil characters appear only late in the book, in the chapter "Chemical Examination." The first is Doctor Pannwitz, who tests Levi's qualifications for the chemical work squad. Levi distills Pannwitz's evil into a single look: "Because that look was not one between two men; and if I had known how completely to explain the nature of that look, which came as if across the glass window of an aquarium between two beings who live in different worlds, I would also have explained the essence of the great insanity of the third Germany."[23] Levi cannot fully articulate that look, but he continues trying:

> One felt in that moment, in an immediate manner, what we all thought and said of the Germans. The brain which governed those blue eyes and those manicured hands said: "This something in front of me belongs to a species which it is obviously opportune to suppress. In this particular case, one has to first make sure that it does not contain some utilizable element." And in my head, like seeds in an empty pumpkin: "Blue

eyes and fair hair are essentially wicked. No communication possible."[24]

Levi's interpretation of Pannwitz is chilling and convincing, but he goes beyond it, and even undermines it, by critiquing his own stereotyping: his crude thoughts, "like seeds in an empty pumpkin," linking evil to "blue eyes and fair hair."

The other evil man in *If This Is A Man* is not a Nazi soldier or administrator, but a fellow prisoner: Alex, a green triangle, a German criminal. Alex has achieved the position of Kapo, which he lords over his fellow inmates. As he takes Levi back from the exam with Pannwitz, Alex grabs hold of a cable that is covered with thick, black grease.

> Without hatred and without sneering, Alex wipes his hand on my shoulder, both the palm and the back of the hand, to clean it; he would be amazed, the poor brute Alex, if someone told him that today, on the basis of this action, I judge him and Pannwitz and the innumerable others like him, big and small, in Auschwitz and everywhere.[25]

How, in the shadow of the gas chambers, could this minute indignity, committed by a fellow inmate, be the key, the standard by which Levi will measure everyone? By using Alex's seemingly trivial act as his scale, Levi shows how easy it is—how casually one can start—to treat others as subhuman, in Auschwitz and "everywhere."

After *If This Is a Man*, Levi remained deeply curious about the Nazis and wrote about them more extensively. He contributed a preface to the memoirs of the commandant of Auschwitz, Rudolf Höss. Höss, he says, was one of the greatest criminals who ever lived, but he was molded from the same clay as a bourgeois person from any other nation.[26] In a different climate, he would have become an anonymous bureaucrat. Höss was not a hate-filled fanatic, writes Levi, but a tranquil and diligent idiot.[27]

In *If Not Now, When?*, the character Mendel offers some thoughts on how ordinary people like Höss become killers and torturers.

> You have to understand the Germans, and I've never managed that. The Germans think a Jew is worth less than a Russian, and a Russian less than an Englishman, and that a German is worth most of all; they think, too, that when one man is worth more than another man, he has the right to do what he likes with the other, make a slave of him or even kill him. Maybe not all of them are convinced, but this is what they're taught in school, and this is what their propaganda says.[28]

As Levi writes in *The Drowned and the Saved*, the Nazis had been reared badly, subjected to a terrible miseducation.[29] The human soul is malleable, particularly in youth, and easily deformed by propaganda.

Even when he did write about the Nazis, Levi shied away from any attempt to *fully* explain them. As he writes in the afterword of a school edition of *If This Is a Man,* "Perhaps one cannot, what is more one must not, understand what happened, because to understand is almost to justify."[30] To understand, one must identify, and no one should identify with Hitler or Eichmann. This insight into the limits of understanding is unusual for a secular, scientific thinker such as Levi. He implies that evil has a contagious, taboo quality: to get too close to unclean things is to become unclean. True understanding requires an act of mimesis, a moral empathy, which it would be dangerous to extend to radical evil.

But if Levi did not believe that a complete understanding of the Nazis was possible, he believed emphatically in judging their actions. He was not interested in blanket condemnations of the German people, but neither was he interested in any kind of blanket forgiveness. He told an interviewer:

> I can only consider justice case by case. If I had had Eichmann in front of me I would have sentenced him to death…Anyone who commits a crime must pay, unless he repents. But not in words. Verbal repentance is not enough. I am disposed to forgive a man who has shown by his actions that he is no longer the man he was. And not too late.[31]

It is possible for the inhuman to become human again—even the inhumanly evil. But it is an arduous task, not accomplished by words alone. Levi did not see the possibility of redemption for Eichmann; what he deserved was endless suffering. As Levi writes in the poem "For Adolf Eichmann":

> May you live sleepless five million nights,
> And may you be visited each night by the suffering of
>   everyone who saw,
> Shutting behind him, the door that blocked the way
>   back…[32]

It is disturbing that Levi wants someone to suffer for five million nights. Yet the punishment seems calibrated quite precisely to the crime.

Levi always distinguished between Nazi leaders and followers. While he never absolved the followers of guilt—the "fear, the desire for profit, the blindness and willed stupidity"—he placed it carefully in context.[33] He did not like it when Germans came to him for forgiveness, particularly if they had done nothing to merit it, but he answered their letters, mastered their language, and took particular care with the German editions of his works. He preserved every letter he received from a German and considered making a whole book of them (he used some in the final chapter of The Drowned and the Saved, "Letters from Germans").[34] Levi wanted to relate to Germans as one human being to another, but he also wanted to confront them with the Nazis' crimes. On business trips to Germany, he sometimes showed his business partners his tattoo, or told them that he had learned German at Auschwitz.

He did not want to stereotype the Germans as the Nazis had stereotyped the Jews. In "Last Christmas of the War," he describes how one of the German women in the lab secretly hired him to fix her bike tire and rewarded him generously with an egg, four lumps of sugar, and the mysterious, absurd, whispered note of encouragement, "Christmas will soon be here." In telling this story forty years later, Levi writes, he is not trying to make excuses for the Nazis. "One human German," he says, "does not whitewash the innumerable inhuman or indifferent ones, but it does have the merit of breaking a stereotype."[35]

Later in life, Levi crafted two detailed portraits of individual Germans, based on real people. Tellingly, he chose men who resembled him: chemists who had worked at Auschwitz. He got information about both men from a German woman named Hety Schmitt-Maas, whose ex-husband had been a chemist for I. G. Farben, the company that ran the factory at the Lager. Schmitt-Maas had begun reading Levi's books and had become an important correspondent and friend. She told him about Reinhard Heidebroek, a colleague of her ex-husband. After the war, Heidebroek began to drink heavily, tormented by his memories of Auschwitz. He read *If This Is a Man* but, in communications with Schmitt-Maas, defended Dr. Pannwitz's behavior toward Levi, which made Levi furious.[36]

Levi was fascinated by Heidebroek and based the memoir-story "The Quiet City" on him, renaming him "Mertens." Interestingly, he told Schmitt-Maas that he did not want to write from a "judgmental point of view (I am no judge, I am no Wiesenthal, and Heidebroek is not a criminal)."[37] He may have been downplaying his intentions, however, given that he was asking Schmitt-Maas to help him get in touch with Heidebroek and would not have wanted to scare either of them off.

Certainly Levi does not eschew judgment in the story, although he judges Mertens thoughtfully. He notes his similarities to Mertens, calling him an "almost-me, another myself, turned upside down."[38] He gives Mertens credit for reading *If This Is a Man*, showing that he is not cynical or insensitive.[39] Mertens does not lie to himself about the past, but he gives himself the gift of blanks, lacunae.[40] Levi renders justice by filling in those blanks: he writes a letter telling Mertens that "if Hitler had risen to power, devastated Europe and brought Germany to ruin, it was because many good German citizens behaved the way he did, trying not to see and keeping silent about what they did see."[41]

Perhaps Levi's most nuanced attempt to reach the truth about an individual German takes place in the chapter "Vanadium" in *The Periodic Table*. Paradoxically, however, this is one of Levi's most fictionalized Auschwitz stories. Levi had read dozens of historical and journalistic accounts of the Nazis, but he remained unsatisfied because, as he put it, the documentary evidence "almost never has the power to give us the depths of a human being; for this purpose the dramatist or poet are more appropriate than the historian or psychologist."[42] Not surprisingly, then, he resorted to fiction to get at the depths in "Vanadium."

Levi asked for Schmitt-Maas' help in tracking down a German chemist from Auschwitz, Dr. Meyer, who, he said, had behaved particularly well, given the circumstances.[43] Schmitt-Maas found Meyer and sent him *If This Is a Man*, along with Levi's address. Meyer wrote to Levi, with an odd blend of moving repentance and self-serving excuses; he asked that they meet. Levi responded, telling Meyer that he had good memories of him and recalling that Meyer had written a note entitling him to be shaved twice a week and to receive a pair of leather shoes and a clean shirt.[44]

In "Vanadium," Levi re-creates Meyer as "Müller." He uses many details taken directly from Meyer's life and what appear to be direct quotations from his letters, but he also creates an entirely fictional frame, in which he rediscovers Müller sometime after the war via business correspondence about a batch of defective resin. Levi writes that he had been dreaming of precisely this moment: "To find myself, man to man, having a reckoning with one of the 'others' had been my keenest and most constant desire since I had left the concentration camp."[45]

Levi's portrait of Meyer as Müller in "Vanadium" was more negative than Schmitt-Maas expected, based on her own meetings with him and what Levi had said about him previously. When she wrote to Levi about this "unkind" transformation,

Levi replied that he had thought it more effective, from a literary point of view, to play down Meyer's redeeming points and make him a typical German corrupted by the Hitler regime.[46] Meyer's widow felt even more strongly about it: she considered suing for defamation. And yet Levi's depiction of Müller seems remarkably even-handed. He assigns him not to the circle of the evil but to the "gray zone."

> Neither infamous nor a hero: after filtering off the rhetoric and the lies in good or bad faith there remained a typically gray human specimen, one of the not so few one-eyed men in the kingdom of the blind....I did not love him, and I didn't want to see him, and yet I felt a certain measure of respect for him: it is not easy to be one-eyed. He was not cowardly, or deaf, or a cynic, he had not conformed, he was trying to settle his accounts with the past and they didn't tally: he tried to make them tally, perhaps by cheating a little bit.[47]

In the story, Müller is part of the silent German majority, whose crime was to know as little as possible and avoid demanding explanations from anyone, even themselves.[48] After the war, he resorts to convenient fictions and probably succeeds in believing them. He takes shelter in commonplaces, and his efforts to overcome the past are "clumsy, a bit ridiculous, irritating and sad, and yet decorous."[49] As the word "decorous" suggests, Levi is far from contemptuous, but he remains suspicious of overcoming.

One of Meyer's letters suggested that Levi had overcome Judaism to reach a Christian state of forgiveness: a supposition Levi found deeply offensive. Levi was not interested in forgiving Meyer, but in balancing the books. But he was subtle enough to do Meyer justice, and he was complex and ironical enough to use fictionalized memories to critique Müller, a fictionalized character, for fictionalizing his memories.

Drowning is perhaps Levi's most central metaphor. The most overt echo is of Dante, who uses "drowned" to refer to the damned souls in hell. But the motif of shipwreck and drowning recurs throughout Levi's life and work: in his love of Melville and Conrad, his traumatic near-drafting by the navy, his translation of "The Ballad of Sir Patrick Spens," and his repeated citations of Samuel Taylor Coleridge's "Rime of the Ancient Mariner," to name but a few examples. In his later writings, Levi uses the image of drowning for people who become lost in a variety of ways, including depression. Even Leonid, one of the heroic partisans in *If Not Now, When?*, is a "shipwrecked boy," suffering from mental trauma.[50]

Most often, Levi uses the word "drowned" to refer to prisoners at Auschwitz who have been so beaten down by the Lager that they have lost their humanity. For Levi, humanity is a mutual, reciprocal creation. If I treat you as inhuman, I forfeit my own humanity. Therefore, it is not surprising that Levi considers evil men like Pannwitz to be less than human. What is shocking, however, is that Levi considers most of his fellow inmates inhuman, too. In *If This Is a Man*, he says that all the drowned have the same story, or, to be more exact, no story. He calls them an anonymous mass of identical non-men, the divine spark dead within them, too empty to really suffer. He concludes:

> They crowd my memory with their faceless presences, and if
> I could enclose all the evil of our time in one image, I would

choose this image which is familiar to me: an emaciated man, with head dropped and shoulders curved, on whose face and in whose eyes not a trace of thought is to be seen.[51]

In other passages of *If This Is a Man*, Levi is even more caustic, describing various inmates as "beasts," "specimens," "scum," "inhuman," or "monsters." His language, so tempered and humane at times, can seem cruel and dehumanizing. But if Levi does not describe most inmates as less than human, his most urgent point is lost. His core idea is not, as the back jacket of the American edition says, "the indestructible human spirit"; it is precisely the opposite: that the human spirit can be quickly demolished when absolute power is combined with a dehumanizing view of others. That is why Levi's "one image" for the evil of our time is not the image of a Nazi, but rather of a Nazi victim.[52]

Levi unmistakably signals his intent by prefacing *If This Is a Man* with the unnerving poem "Shemà," in which he asks us to consider whether the Nazis' victims were still men when they labored in the mud and fought for crusts of bread, their eyes empty.[53] Levi radically rewrites the most basic Jewish prayer, the Shemà, God's call to Israel. His words, he tells us, are so important that we must engrave them on our hearts every hour of the day. If we do not, Levi curses us, asking that our houses crumble, diseases afflict us, and our children reject us. It is striking, to say the least, to assign such importance to one's own words. And yet, for all his ambition, Levi is never vainglorious. He is using every ounce of poetic and moral authority to force us to "consider whether this is a man."[54] If we simply assume the humanity of the Nazis' victims, we have failed as his readers.

As Levi writes in a later essay, "There is nothing honorable about slavery." It is "essentially ignoble, the fount of almost irresistible degradation and moral shipwreck."[55] This does not mean lumping victims and assassins together. It means that the guilt of the Nazis is a hundred times greater, for having destroyed not just bodies but also souls.[56] Never before had anyone created a process of brutalization to demolish the human part of men even before killing them.[57] Yet, while Levi focuses blame squarely on the Nazis, at times his descriptions of the victims seem not only judgmental but also contemptuous.

One can find some personal factors in Levi's contempt for the anonymous mass of his fellow inmates. The vast majority of the prisoners were Eastern European Jews, and, at the time of his internment at Auschwitz, Levi held some of the common Italian prejudices against them as being provincial, poor, uncultured, and obscurantist. Many Italian Jews, such as Levi's father, blamed the Eastern Jews for inciting hostility against Jews everywhere with their backward ways.[58] The hostility was mutual: according to *If This Is a Man*, the Polish Jews despised the Italian Jews.[59] As Levi elaborated in an interview:

> The contact I had there with Eastern Judaism was traumatic and negative. We were rejected, as Sephardi or in any case Italian Jews, because we didn't speak Yiddish, we were doubly foreign...we were not part of their world, they had not the slightest idea that there was any other Judaism...A great many of the Polish Jews who were of humble origin were angered by our presence: "but what sort of Jew are you?...they would say....A *jid* who doesn't speak *jiddisch* isn't a *jid*."[60]

Levi portrays some Eastern Jews favorably in *If This Is a Man*: for example, Chajim, his Polish bed-mate, whom he trusts blindly; and Mendi, a modernist rabbi, Zionist, lawyer, and partisan who speaks seven languages: a stubborn and courageous little man.[61] But having been rejected by the Eastern Jews, Levi naturally tended to reject them, and that may be one of the reasons that the bulk of the prisoners, the drowned, were so faceless to him. Occasionally his hostility (and elitism) manifests itself directly: he refers to the dwarf Elias as speaking only "the surly and deformed Yiddish of Warsaw."[62]

Levi offers hints of how things could have been different if he had understood Yiddish: if, for example, he had understood the words of the rhapsody sung by the storyteller at night, probably encompassing all of Lager life in minute detail.[63] He tells us about Rabbi Wachsmann: a thin, soft, fragile man who lights up with an amazing vitality as he discusses Talmudic questions.[64] Perhaps, if Levi had spoken Yiddish, some of these songs and conversations would have helped to humanize and differentiate the drowned. Perhaps, but Levi's identification with the Eastern Jews would have to wait until years later, when he taught himself Yiddish and wrote *If Not Now, When?* about heroic, East European Jewish partisans. (As if in compensation, the novel is set in precisely the same time period as *If This Is a Man*: 1943–1945.)

In addition to his Italian insularity and secularism, Levi brought to Auschwitz an already-hardened view of the struggle for life—not just from his mountaineering and his readings of Darwin, Conrad, Melville, and London, but also from surviving the Chemistry Institute under the direction of Professor Ponzio. Just as he had been one of eighty candidates striving to be chemist specialists at Auschwitz (only three of whom made it to the relative safety of the lab), so he had been one of eighty chemistry students, of whom only thirty graduated.[65] His description of Ponzio's Institute, using terms like "natural selection," makes it sound like a weird rehearsal for Auschwitz. That is why it is bizarre, but not completely surprising, to hear Levi refer to the deaths of the drowned as a "process of natural selection."[66] On one level, Levi knows that the selections are not natural: they are the most man-made evil of all time. But on another level he finds such brutality natural because he finds nature brutal.

Levi had cultivated the hard objectivity of a scientist. Part of him looked on at the Lager as "pre-eminently a gigantic biological and social experiment."[67] Too much sympathy for the drowned men would not only endanger his life (because he had no bread, no energy, no time to spare), but also his scientific detachment, with which he hoped to learn "what is essential and what adventitious to the conduct of the human animal in the struggle for life."[68] Levi is aware of the irony—and to some readers, perhaps, the offensiveness—of a survivor calling the Lager an "experiment"; but he is brave enough not to disguise his feelings, or his lack of feelings.

In his theoretical quest to understand what it means to be human, Levi finds it useful to have counter-examples: nonhuman humans. To put it another way, Levi's secular philosophy is premised on the notion that man's essence, his humanity, is not a preordained gift from God; rather, it is something that man himself must create, cultivate, and safeguard. If his philosophy is true, then it must include examples of people who never acquire, or who lose, their humanity.

Levi's apparent inhumanity also accurately reflects the attitude that many prisoners had toward each other and themselves. It was not just the Nazis who referred to the inmates
as "pieces" and animals. The prisoners referred to their own
eating as *fressen*, the word for animals eating, rather than *essen*,
the word for humans eating, because, Levi writes, it was exactly
the right word for eating "on our feet, furiously, burning our
mouths and throats, without time to breathe."[69] The prisoners recognized their own animality, just as they recognized
that too much time spent pitying or humanizing the drowned
endangered their own survival.

The drowned are hard to describe. They are, by definition,
the unmemorable ones, the ones who fail to exert their personalities enough to seem human. Levi refers to his first exemplar
of the drowned only by his number—and the German version
of his number, at that:

> He is Null Achtzehn. He is not called anything except that,
> Zero Eighteen, the last three figures of his entry number; as
> if everyone was aware that only man is worthy of a name,
> and that Null Achtzehn is no longer a man. I think that even
> he has forgotten his name, certainly he acts as if this was so.
> When he speaks, when he looks around, he gives the impres-
> sion of being empty inside, nothing more than an involucre,
> like the slough of certain insects which one finds on the banks
> of swamps, held by a thread to the stones and shaken by the
> wind.[70]

Levi tells us that Null Achtzehn is very young, that he carries
out all the orders he is given, that he works too hard and thus
makes a dangerous companion, and that he is so indifferent that
he does not even trouble to avoid blows. This youth, in Levi's

eyes, has forfeited his humanity not by being evil or depraved, but by going like a sheep to be slaughtered. He makes Levi think of the sled-dogs in Jack London's stories, slaving until the last breath and dying on the track.[71]

Levi hates Null Achtzehn for letting the Nazis win so easily, but he also hates him for being a potential version of himself—because, as it turns out, he and Null Achtzehn have some frailties in common. As Levi explains, no one wants to work with him, either, because he is weak and clumsy, and so he often gets paired with Null.[72] In fact, when Levi arrived at Auschwitz, he looked like someone who would drown. His bunkmate, Maurice Reznik, later recalled, "His physical frailty struck me at once, and I knew that if he didn't get help he wouldn't last long."[73] One day, because Levi could not carry the railway ties on his own, Reznik helped him, taking nearly all the load: "Others would have rejected him because he was too small," explained Reznik, "but this was a matter of life or death."[74]

Even more dangerously, at first Levi spoke only a little German, learned from studying chemistry, and no Yiddish or Polish.[75] According to one source, Levi was saved from immediate extermination only because his friend Alberto Dalla Volta told the Germans—in German—that he was a chemist and that Levi was his assistant.[76] Levi writes in *If This is a Man* that, even after some time in the Lager, he was sometimes convinced that he would drown: "I know that I am not made of the stuff of those who resist, I am too civilized, I still think too much, I use myself up at work."[77] But he did resist, and he used his intellect to help his chances of survival: passing a chemical exam to get an inside job, craftily stealing from the Nazis, and buying German lessons from his friend Jean.

Toward the end of his imprisonment, Levi—both as character and narrator—can spare more pity for the drowned. He memorializes a drowning man, Kraus, not only providing his name but even naming a chapter of *If This Is a Man* after him. Kraus, like Null Achtzehn, is a naïve young man who works too hard and acts as if normal rules still applied. His German is poor, and he cannot understand or make himself understood. As Levi puts it, "What a good boy Kraus must have been as a civilian: he will not survive very long here, one can see it at the first glance, it is as logical as a theorem."[78] But Levi, who has told us that it is a mistake—a waste of effort and prestige—to talk to the drowned, invents a consoling fiction for Kraus, telling him that he has had a dream in which they are in Italy, warm, well-fed, and happy.[79] Levi, at this point in the narrative, feels more like a man and less like a Null; hence his contempt for the boyish Kraus is leavened with pity.

Similarly, in a story written years later, "Rappoport's Testament," Levi presents a detailed picture of one of the drowned, Valerio, and rescues him from anonymity. Valerio falls into the mud constantly, unlike most of the men, who at least try not to fall, thanks to "that bit of animal nobility that survives even in a man reduced to despair."[80] In this passage, as in *If This Is a Man*, Levi describes the typical inmate as a despairing animal, but this time animality is not the opposite of humanity; instead, animal nobility is part of man's dignity, and most men try not to fall. Even though Valerio welcomes oblivion and falls into the mud, Levi still gives him a name, an identity, and a measure of sympathy—far more than he had been willing to give Null Achtzehn. Levi even allows him to become an artist of sorts, describing how

Valerio recounts his misadventures and dramatizes them
with theatrical flamboyance.[81]

Drawing again on Dante, Levi often contrasts the "drowned"
with the "saved." In Dante's terminology, the "saved" are the
opposite of the damned; they are the ones who win eternal life
with God. In Levi's universe, the "saved" correspond loosely
to the survivors, but, as Levi makes clear, bodily and moral
survival are two very different things. The Nazis created a
Hobbesian inferno in which man was a wolf to man, everyone
either an enemy or a rival.[82] As Levi told an interviewer:

> This was the human material I had around me. Among these
> unfortunates, there was no solidarity, none at all, and this lack
> was the first and biggest trauma. I and the others who'd been
> transported with me had thought, naively, "However bad it
> may be, we'll find comrades." It didn't turn out that way. We
> found enemies, not comrades.[83]

The law of the Lager was to eat your own bread, and if you
could, that of your neighbor.[84] To save yourself, you had to
dodge work, find influential friends, hide thoughts, steal, and
lie.[85] Far from being saints, the saved occupied a "gray zone":
neither pure oppressors nor pure victims.

Levi's distinction between drowned and saved is not stable,
and it is not the same as the distinction between inhuman and
human. He humanizes some of the drowned, like Kraus and
Valerio, and he dehumanizes many of the saved. In fact, the
four examples of saved men he gives in *If This Is a Man* are each
described as less than human. Schepschel has learned to think

of himself only as "a sack which needs periodic refilling," and he does not hesitate to betray a fellow inmate.[86] Alfred L. behaves with absolute egotism; he lives the "cold life of the determined and joyless dominator."[87] Elias, the dwarf, is compared to a monkey, a wild animal, a stone, a piece of wood, and a monster—all in the space of two pages.[88] And Henri, eminently civilized and sane, is compared to a cat and then described as "intent on his hunt…the enemy of all, inhumanly cunning and incomprehensible like the Serpent in Genesis."[89]

Why are these saved men less than men? Because they have accepted the basic premise of the Nazi experiment: that they are completely alone, at war with all others, and can survive only by using other men like things. They are not sheep, but they are wolves. After the war, when an old friend suggested that Levi's survival was the work of Providence, Levi responded bitterly. As he explains in *The Drowned and the Saved*:

> Such an opinion seemed monstrous to me. It pained me as when one touches an exposed nerve, and kindled the doubt I spoke of before: I might be alive in the place of another, at the expense of another; I might have usurped, that is, in fact, killed. The "saved" of the Lager were not the best, those predestined to do good, the bearers of a message: what I had seen and lived through proved the exact contrary. Preferably the worst survived, the selfish, the violent, the insensitive, the collaborators of the "gray zone," the spies. It was not a certain rule (there were none, nor are there certain rules in human matters), but it was nevertheless a rule. I felt innocent, yes, but enrolled among the saved and therefore in permanent search of a justification in my own eyes and those of others. The worst survived, that is, the fittest; the best all died.[90]

Maybe in Ponzio's university lab, the fittest were the best, but at Auschwitz "natural selection" was much different. In normal life, a man can exert his vitality, power, and love of life without necessarily hurting others. But in the zero-sum world of Auschwitz, all power was antagonistic. The basic food ration did not sustain life; the inmates had to collaborate or steal to survive.

Stealing—even from the Nazis—did not come easily to Levi. In *The Periodic Table,* he notes that if you do not begin to steal as a child, it is hard to learn. It took him several months to repress the moral commandments, but, eventually, like the dog Buck in *The Call of the Wild,* he stole with sly cunning at every opportunity—everything except the bread of his companions.[91] Although he did not steal from other inmates, he still felt guilty, because every bite of food he ate was a bite that could have helped keep someone else alive. Even sleeping was an ordeal, as the Nazis forced the prisoners to sleep two to a bunk, on mattresses too small to fit both men. In *If This Is a Man,* Levi describes how his bunkmate, whose face he had barely seen, used to push him aside with a blow from his bony hips.[92]

As the Nazis destroyed the souls of the drowned, they also corrupted the souls of the saved, especially those who collaborated in some way, however small: the Kapos, camp elders, messengers, bed makers—all of the so-called prominents who gained some official status that helped them survive. In *If This Is a Man,* Levi recalls his and others' amazement that the first blows they felt in the Lager came not from SS officers but from the prominents. He theorizes that the prominents hated the Nazis but could not lash out at them; as a result they discharged their violent hatred onto those below them.[93]

The Nazis had various practical reasons for corrupting the inmates: to prevent revolts, for example, and to obtain free labor to administer the Lager. They also felt the psychological need to prove that their victims were subhuman and to shift some of the guilt onto them. In his preface to J. Presser's *Night of the Girondins,* Levi writes that evil is contagious. The man who is a non-man "dehumanizes others, every crime radiates outward and takes root all around, corrupting consciences and surrounding itself with accomplices won over by fear or seduction."[94]

In *The Drowned and the Saved,* Levi cites a host of reasons why the inhabitants of the gray zone acted as they did. He notes the effects of ghettoization, fatigue, humiliation, isolation, the death of loved ones, Nazi brutality, and the simple desire for survival. Speaking more generally about gray zones everywhere, he lists "terror, ideological seduction, servile imitation of the victor, myopic desire for any power whatsoever, even though ridiculously circumscribed in space and time, cowardice, and, finally, lucid calculation aimed at eluding the imposed orders and order."[95] He explains the vying for prestige and the need to create a *we* at the expense of a *they.* In an interview with Ferdinando Camon, Levi stresses the effect of the removal of law: "Particularly where law turns out to be lacking, the law of the jungle is established, Darwinian law, by which the fittest, who are mostly the worst, prevail and survive by eating the living flesh of the others."[96]

In his more positive moods, Levi has a certain admiration for the vitality of the stronger beasts. In introducing his later collection of Lager stories, *Moments of Reprieve,* he praises his protagonists, however immoral, as authentic men. They are not the anonymous, faceless, voiceless mass of the shipwrecked, but the few in whom he had seen, if only for a moment, free will, and hence a rudiment of virtue.[97] In "Rappoport's Testament," he describes Rappoport as a tiger in the jungle, preying on the weak, ready to corrupt, steal, fight, or flatter, depending on the situation. But he also offers Rappoport a measure of nobility, comparing him to Capaneus, a warrior in the seventh circle of Dante's Hell, who shouts out insults at Jove and laughs at his thunderbolts.

Rappoport is a man, even if he is a bad man. In the *Moments of Reprieve* stories, Levi uses a more elastic definition of humanity than in *If This Is a Man.* Not coincidentally, the literary style in these stories is different, too. They read more like fiction and less like memoir, essay, or sociological study. Levi gives the characters fuller physical descriptions and many more lines of dialogue; he allows them to speak for themselves, convey their own "testaments."[98] In these stories, even a German criminal can be shown performing a good deed: in "The Juggler," Eddie the Kapo, a pederast and former street thief, spares Levi from denunciation when he finds him writing a letter. Levi wonders what kind of humanity Eddie and the other green triangles possessed and regrets that no one from that "ambiguous brigade" has yet told his story.[99]

Levi further explores the ambiguity of the gray zone in "Story of a Coin," a historical meditation on Chaim Rumkowski, a Jewish man who made himself the overlord of the Lodz ghetto:

> Paradoxically, his identification with the oppressor is flanked by, or perhaps alternates with, an identification with the

oppressed, because man, as Thomas Mann says, is a confused creature. And he becomes even more confused, we may add, when he is subjected to extreme tensions: he then eludes our judgment, the way a compass needle goes wild at the magnetic pole.[100]

What is true of Rumkowski, Levi writes, is true of all of us; we are "so dazzled by power and prestige as to forget our essential fragility."[101] This type of existential thinking—attributing such behaviors to basic human attributes, rather than to Nazi dehumanization—is less prevalent in *If This Is a Man*, in which Levi seems to feel a stronger obligation to document the Nazis' crimes. But even in the earlier book, the gray zone is not confined to Auschwitz, but is a part of life in general: "[I]t is in the normal order of things that the privileged oppress the unprivileged."[102]

In judging the inhabitants of the gray zone, Levi draws Dantean distinctions between the low-level functionaries—sweepers, kettle washers, night watchmen, bed smoothers, and checkers of lice—and those in commanding positions: Kapos, barracks chiefs, clerks, and elders.[103] Among the Kapos, he distinguishes between common criminals, political prisoners broken by years of suffering, Jews seeing their only option of escaping death, sadists, frustrated lovers of power, and contaminated victims. When it comes to the inmates forced to work in the crematoriums, Levi discusses their moral dilemmas at length, and then asks us to meditate on their story with pity and rigor, but also to suspend our judgment.[104]

In all his work, Levi is more interested in the moral degradation created by the Nazis than in the destruction of Jewish culture or the physical torment. While distinguishing clearly between victimizers and victims, he never sanctifies the victims. As he writes in *The Drowned and the Saved*, "It is naïve, absurd, and historically false to believe that an infernal system such as National Socialism was, sanctifies its victims: on the contrary, it degrades them, makes them resemble itself, and this all the more when they are available, blank, and lack a political or moral armature."[105]

Some prisoners maintained a moral armature that might be called "discipline" or the "care of the self." Levi describes it in the chapter of *If This Is a Man* titled "The Initiation." He is in the washroom with his friend Steinlauf, a middle-aged, former soldier who had won an Iron Cross serving the Austro-Hungarian Empire in the First World War. Steinlauf asks Levi severely why he does not wash. Levi responds that washing one's face in the Lager is "a stupid feat, even frivolous: a mechanical habit, or worse, a dismal repetition of an extinct rite." If he has ten spare minutes, he would rather use them for personal reflection or simply look up at the sky.[106] Steinlauf then "administers" Levi a "complete lesson":

> It grieves me now that I have forgotten his plain, outspoken
> words...It grieves me because it means that I have to trans-
> late his uncertain Italian and his quiet manner of speaking of
> a good soldier into my language of an incredulous man. But
> this was the sense, not forgotten either then or later: that pre-
> cisely because the Lager was a great machine to reduce us to
> beasts, we must not become beasts; that even in this place one
> can survive, and therefore one must want to survive, to tell
> the story, to bear witness; and that to survive we must force

ourselves to save at least the skeleton, the scaffolding, the form of civilization.[107]

At first, the reader might think that this is indeed a "complete lesson," a magnificent summa. But Levi has already undercut Steinlauf slightly, with the unattractive word "administers" and with the irony of a "good soldier" from the Austro-Hungarian army discoursing to Levi, an "incredulous" man. Levi's forgetting of Steinlauf's words is itself ambiguous; it allows Levi to render them in his own eloquent words, but it also suggests that the original speech was not memorable.

Still, nothing can prepare us for the surprise that Levi accepts this beautiful lesson "only in part":

> These things Steinlauf, a man of good will, told me; strange things to my unaccustomed ear, understood and accepted only in part, and softened by an easier, more flexible and blander doctrine, which for centuries has found its dwelling place on the other side of the Alps; according to which, among other things, nothing is of greater vanity than to force oneself to swallow whole a moral system elaborated by others, under another sky. No, the wisdom and virtue of Steinlauf, certainly good for him, is not enough for me. In the face of this complicated world my ideas of damnation are confused; is it really necessary to elaborate a system and put it into practice? Or would it not be better to acknowledge one's lack of a system?[108]

Levi admires Steinlauf's self-discipline, and, to some extent, he adopts it, but, at the same time, he is repelled by it because Steinlauf, rather than creating it himself, absorbed it from the authoritarian army that trained him. Steinlauf, the good soldier, lacks true individuality; and perhaps that is why Levi has forgotten his words. Even more radically, Levi questions whether any system is adequate for this complicated world, whether any cosmos that is systematic can be true.

Although Steinlauf makes no mention of religion in justifying his ablutions, "The Initiation" reflects many of Levi's attitudes toward religion and the "dismal repetition" of any "extinct rite." Steinlauf represents all those who resist the Nazis by adhering faithfully to a competing system, whether that system is military discipline, Marxism, Christianity, or Judaism. One can tell that Steinlauf is something of a stand-in for the pious, who are mostly absent from *If This Is a Man*, because Levi's response does not quite fit Steinlauf's lecture: Steinlauf's bare principles of self-care and dignity are hardly an entire moral system that must be swallowed whole.

In later stories and essays, Levi elaborates on his ambiguous feelings toward those who guard their humanity with faith. He notes, for example, that believers of any kind "lived better" in the Lager, because of the saving force of their faith:

> Their universe was vaster than ours, more extended in space and time, above all more comprehensible: they had a key and a point of leverage, a millennial tomorrow so that there might be a sense to sacrificing themselves, a place in heaven or on earth where justice and compassion had won, or would win in a perhaps remote but certain future: Moscow, or the celestial or terrestrial Jerusalem. Their hunger was different from ours. It was a divine punishment or expiation, or votive offering, or the fruit of capitalist putrefaction. Sorrow, in them or around them, was decipherable and therefore did not overflow into despair.[109]

Levi exhibits scorn for believers by lumping them all together, from Stalinists to Orthodox Jews, but also displays a certain envy and admiration. The phrase "lived better" might mean that their delusions made them happier, but it might also mean that their faith made them better people.

Interestingly, in the later stories published in *Moments of Reprieve*, Levi sometimes praises nonreligious characters with religious terms. Lorenzo, an atheist, is "like a savior who's come from heaven."[110] Bandi, an innocent and good young Hungarian, is Levi's "disciple"; Levi says that his last name, Szántó, is pronounced like *santo* in Italian, reinforcing the impression that "a halo seemed to encircle his shaved head."[111] He compares Bandi, an atheistic Communist, to both pious Hassidim and proto-Christians.[112]

Conversely, Levi sometimes criticizes characters who really *are* religious as selfish. In *If This Is a Man,* an inmate named Kuhn thanks God for sparing him from the selection while sitting right next to Beppo the Greek, who has been marked for extermination. Levi says that if he were God, he would spit at Kuhn's prayer.[113] However unfairly, Levi finds the religious characters both too selfless—in swallowing another's system—and too selfish, in their care for themselves. In an interview, he describes his own attempt to pray in Auschwitz as a "religious temptation." During a mass selection for the gas chambers, he tried, for a moment, to pray, but then said to himself, "No, you can't do this, you don't have the right."[114]

Levi circled back to the question of religion throughout his life. He once told an interviewer, "There is Auschwitz, and so there cannot be God." But his feelings were more ambiguous than his logical language might suggest. On the transcript of the interview, Levi penciled in a fascinating note: "I don't find a solution to this dilemma. I keep looking, but I don't find it."[115] Asked if he was a believer, he answered, "I'd like to be, but I don't succeed."[116] Levi placed the Book of Job first in *The Search for Roots*, wrote a beautiful poem called "Passover," and titled *If Not Now, When?* after a saying of Rabbi Hillel: he never simply "wrote off" religion.

Levi never became observant, but he grew increasingly interested in Judaism over the years. Although it was anti-Semitism, particularly the Racial Laws and his deportation to Auschwitz, that first impressed his Jewish identity upon him, he later cultivated it in a more positive way, particularly when researching and writing *If Not Now, When?*. Not coincidentally, however, this novel is one of his weaker works, somewhat conventional when compared to his deeper and more surprising memoirs, essays, stories, and poems. Levi's work includes rich veins of Jewish culture, but his cosmos is not a Jewish one.

Levi is particularly distant from religion's mystical aspects. He does not delight in the ineffable: when he describes something as lying at the limits of language, it is almost always something bad, such as the Nazi demolition of humanity. He does not pursue an ecstatic union with the uncanny, and when he contemplates the universe as a whole, he tends to perceive it as alien and hostile, something to be conquered. He does not seek what Freud calls the "oceanic feeling"; as we have seen, Levi's greatest fear is being "drowned." Levi did experience feelings of awe and wonder. As a friend said, he had "a gift for observation and an almost religious sense of wonder at the world."[117] But, as the quote suggests, the wonder was linked to observation; it was the wonder of one who contemplates and studies, not the wonder of one who dissolves himself.

It is interesting to compare Levi's Auschwitz stories with the Lager stories that Fred Wander tells in his autobiographical novel *The Seventh Well*. Wander, too, was an atheist, but he was also a Yiddish-speaking Galician with a deep interest in the lost worlds of the Eastern European Jews, as well as an ecstatic love of nature. Levi's title, *If This Is a Man*, comes from his own, secular "Shemà." Wander's title, by contrast, comes from a poem by Rabbi Loew. He saturates his book with images, stories, and figures from Judaism, particularly mystical Hasidism. Wander focuses not so much on the Nazi demolition of man as on the resources—creative, cultural, and mystical—with which the Jews resisted that demolition, even as they were being murdered. Wander could not have written his book without a mystic's sense of another reality: the possibility of a mysterious communion with one's comrades and nature even during degradation. Levi lacks that mystical attitude, and yet he shares with Wander a sense of the sacredness of human relations, especially friendship.

Primo Levi enjoyed many close friendships throughout his life. Friends were particularly important in the formative years of his youth when, apart from the tragic interlude with Vanda Maestro, he had yet to experience a serious romantic relationship. In those years, friendship was Levi's best way to learn firsthand about other people, to shape and be shaped by them. He was drawn to people unlike him, and, despite his confidence in his own judgment, he was remarkably open to seeing the world from their perspectives. In Auschwitz, friendship was one of the things that kept Levi alive, physically and morally.

Alberto Dalla Volta, a fellow chemist from Italy, was Levi's best friend at Auschwitz. Alberto was more than a friend; he was almost an alter ego. As Levi describes him in *Moments of Reprieve*:

> Alberto was my age, had the same build, temperament, and profession as I, and we slept in the same bunk. We even looked somewhat alike; the foreign comrades and the Kapo considered it superfluous to distinguish between us....We were interchangeable, so to speak, and anyone would have predicted for us two the same fate.[118]

Alberto's virtue was to fight bravely for survival, with a cunning more Odyssean than Machiavellian. Levi writes in *If This Is a Man* that Alberto recognized before anyone that life was war but still remained everybody's friend. He understood mankind: he knew "whom to corrupt, whom to avoid, whose compassion to arouse, whom to resist." [119] And yet Alberto never became corrupt: as Levi puts it, the weapons of night were blunted against him.[120]

Alberto and Levi are among the few sympathetic characters in *If This Is a Man* in large part because of their friendship, the way they take care of each other. Alberto is a double, an alter ego, but he is also a complement, a symbiont: he is more practical, confident, and worldly. Alberto's astuteness at procuring food saves Levi's life, and Levi learns from him how to be more crafty. But Levi has mixed feelings about this astuteness and symbiosis, which he expresses in an anecdote in *The Drowned and the Saved.* Once, he and Alberto find a secret source of water and share it with each other but not with a fellow prisoner. This prisoner, Daniele, gives Levi a reproachful look and later, after the liberation, asks him the terrible question: "Why you two and not me?"[121]

Levi feels at once justified and guilty; one cannot save everyone, but Auschwitz creates a terrible double bind: one has to ignore what in normal life would be a basic duty to a neighbor. As he described it in an interview,

> I myself occasionally fraternized with the "drowned" at Auschwitz. But not often. Usually one just let them drift by on their way to death. There was no point in lending a helping hand to those beyond help. The Good Samaritan ethic had no place in the Lager.[122]

What little solidarity existed in the Lager was confined to compatriots.[123] As a member of the tiny Italian population, Levi was acutely aware of the lack of any broader camaraderie. The sense of each stranger as a potential friend was overwhelmed by the sense of each stranger as a potential enemy—or, at the least, a competitor for the resources needed to survive.

The bitter truth is that not a single inmate in *If This Is a Man* is fully human. Levi and Alberto may seem like men, but in the chapter "The Last One," they, too, are demoted. Levi first describes three brave exploits in which he and Alberto organize their survival and win the respect of their peers—stealing brooms, cheating the tool master, creating a complicated scheme to win ten bread rations. Even the serpentine Henri is impressed and starts to treat them on equal terms—although, given Levi's contempt for Henri, that is an ambiguous sign.[124]

As in so many of his stories, Levi follows a humanizing triumph with a dehumanizing defeat. He describes the hanging of an inmate who had taken part in a prisoners' revolt, blowing up a crematorium. The doomed man cries out, "I am the last one!"—meaning the last of the rebels, but also meaning the last real man. The inmates watching, including Levi and Alberto, do not respond; they are the worn-out, the slaves.[125] Back in their hut, Levi and Alberto eat the soup they have stolen, but they cannot look at one another for shame—for having been so docile, for having let the Germans destroy their manhood. They have cared for each other and cheated death, but further than that, their humanity cannot go. They have not been able to care for others, nor have they staged a revolt.

Levi reprises this theme in the final chapter, "The Story of Ten Days," when he describes his friendship with two French Resistance fighters named Charles and Arthur. The Germans have just fled the Lager, and, in this new freedom, the three friends can care not just for each other but also for the other inmates in their hut. Yet when the inmate named Sómogyi dies, Levi refers to him in dehumanizing terms as "the shameful wreck of skin and bones, the Sómogyi thing."[126] To understand how Levi is damning himself, one has to reread a passage several paragraphs prior, in which Levi asserts that the Germans, even as they were defeated, had completed their work of bestial degradation.[127] He goes on to address his central preoccupation with what makes a man:

> It is man who kills, man who creates or suffers injustice; it is
> no longer man who, having lost all restraint, shares his bed
> with a corpse. Whoever waits for his neighbor to die in order

to take his piece of bread is, albeit guiltless, further from the model of the thinking man than the most primitive pigmy or the most vicious sadist.[128]

Because people are inherently social, with souls that overlap, no one can remain pure in the Lager. As Levi phrases it:

> Part of our existence lies in the feelings of those near to us. This is why the experience of someone who has lived for days during which man was merely a thing in the eyes of man is non-human.[129]

The friendship among Levi, Charles, and Arthur grants them only partial immunity from this plague. They, too, wait for Sómogyi to die before dividing up his bread. They do not share a bed with a corpse, but they share a hut with one: when Sómogyi dies during the night, they wait until morning to carry him out, and even then they tend first to more practical needs—emptying the latrine. By calling Sómogyi's corpse a "thing," Levi shows emphatically that he, too, has been infected with inhumanity.

The reader may be inclined to protest. Levi and his Lager friends might be flawed humans, degraded by the Nazi regime, but are they not still human and, in fact, profoundly good? The very shame felt by Levi and Alberto at the hanging is proof of their abiding morality, as is the fact that, as soon as Levi, Charles, and Arthur can help some other inmates, they do. It would be utterly unrealistic to require moral perfection as a precondition to humanity.

Levi himself is not always so rigid in his denial of the inmates' humanity. In *Moments of Reprieve*, Levi focuses on more autonomous, if not always more appealing, characters. Each of these stories, Levi tells us, is centered on a character who "never is the persecuted, predestined victim, the prostrate man, the person to whom I had devoted my first book, and about whom I had obsessively asked myself if this was still a man."[130] Instead, these characters, says Levi, are, "beyond all doubt," men. If they are men, then the apparent thesis of *If This Is a Man*, that the Nazis demolished every man in Auschwitz, turns out to be more a provisional, polemical, literary, and ambiguous proposition than a sociological truth.

The *Moments of Reprieve* stories, Levi explained in an interview, would have seemed out of place in *If This Is a Man*, where he felt that the note of indignation should prevail, because it was "testimony, almost juridical in form."[131] In the later stories, altruism is more common. For example, Tischler makes Levi a present of half an apple, and Bandi, the young Hungarian, brings him a radish. To have included episodes like this in the earlier book would have offered more hope, but it would have lessened the Nazis' crime and blurred Levi's thesis.

Levi leaves the question of the inmates' humanity ambiguous. Even within *If This Is a Man*, he suggests several times that some of the inmates are still men. Once he mentions that there are a "very few superior individuals, made of the stuff of martyrs or saints," who survive without renouncing any part of their moral world.[132] In another passage he says that while most inmates are beasts broken by blows, there are a few who still have appropriate feelings and judgments.[133] While he sometimes lumps himself in with the drowned, at other times he suggests that he remained a man.

Without such ambiguity, Levi would not involve the reader so deeply in thinking about the Lager and human nature. In the opening poem, "Shemà," Levi does not enjoin the reader to consider the demolition of man as a fait accompli. Rather, he commands the reader to consider if this is a man. Levi also complicates things by playing three overlapping roles in his memoirs: author, narrator, and character. Because one finds Levi as author and narrator to be not just a man, but an exemplary man, one finds it hard to think any less of Levi the character. Perhaps Levi would respond that during Auschwitz he was not a man, but that, at times—as a friend, a chemist, a reciter of Dante, a recipient of goodness—he was able to recall (or discover) what it meant to be one.

For those outside the Lager, it was still possible to be a man. Lorenzo Perone was a civilian mason from Italy, conscripted to work at Auschwitz but allowed to live outside it. He was a 40-year-old laborer who had grown up in intense poverty—quiet and withdrawn, given to drink and fighting, but also ethical and kind.[134] One day in June 1944, after Levi had been at Auschwitz for about four months, he was sent to work with Lorenzo and managed to exchange a few words with him. After that, although they met only a few more times, Lorenzo smuggled soup to Levi every other day for six months and thus saved his life. Here is Levi's beautiful attempt to do Lorenzo justice:

> …it was really due to Lorenzo that I am alive today; and not so much for his material aid, as for his having constantly reminded me by his presence, by his natural and plain manner

of being good, that there still existed a just world outside our own, something and someone still pure and whole, not corrupt, not savage, extraneous to hatred and terror; something difficult to define, a remote possibility of good, but for which it was worth surviving.[135]

The other figures in his book, Levi says, are not men. Their humanity was lost in the crimes they committed or suffered. Only Lorenzo was able to keep his humanity pure and uncontaminated, and so, as Levi puts it, "Thanks to Lorenzo, I managed not to forget that I myself was a man."[136]

Lorenzo exemplifies a primary component of Levi's concept of virtue: care for others. He does the most basic duty, the one first performed by a mother: he feeds someone. This type of goodness is central to Judeo-Christian tradition, but here Levi manages to express it without falling back on religious language. He makes goodness the touchstone of what it means to be a man. Lorenzo's goodness not only makes him a man; it also reminds Levi that he is a man, at least potentially. In other words, one person's humanity helps to generate another's.

Levi makes this point clear by comparing his relationship with Lorenzo to the relationships that other prisoners have with civilian "patrons" who smuggle them food or goods. The other relationships are tainted by the self-interest of the patrons, who, unlike Lorenzo, receive something of value from the inmates. They are tainted by the inmates themselves, who, unlike Levi, bargain with or seduce their allies. Levi is repulsed by the way that the inmates discuss their conquests, like men of the world discussing their romantic adventures.[137]

The most professional seducer in *If This Is a Man* is Henri, the snake-like inmate with the "delicate and subtly perverse body and face of Sodoma's San Sebastian." Levi implies that Henri is gay by comparing him with a popular homosexual icon, the arrow-pierced Saint Sebastian painted by Giovanni "Sodoma" Bazzi in 1527.[138] What troubles Levi, however, is not so much Henri's homosexuality as *any* sexuality. For Levi, a pure relationship requires the asexual goodness of the caring comrade, the Kantian, disinterested goodness of giving without receiving.

Lorenzo's goodness is combined with other Levian virtues. He is brave: he could be put in the Lager himself if caught. He is skeptical: he is not a believer and does not know much about the Gospel.[139] He is self-effacing: Levi later learns that Lorenzo had helped other inmates too, and not just Italians, but that he thought it right not to talk about it. Levi, whose raison d'être was to write about his own life, had a deep respect for those who, in his words, did not "do things in order to talk about them (like me)."[140]

Levi admires the way Lorenzo cannot bear to do anything but good work as a mason, even when working for the Nazis. He respects Lorenzo's autonomy, the way he stubbornly lives his own way. In the story "Lorenzo's Return," published in *Moments of Reprieve*, Levi tells how, when the war ends, Lorenzo walks all the way home to Italy. When he bumps into his cousin in a cart, six kilometers from home, he turns down a ride; he wants to finish his journey as he began it, on foot.[141] Later, he stops working as a mason and becomes a scrap dealer because he wants nothing to do with rules, bosses, or schedules.[142]

Levi fills out the portrait with personal details he would not publish when Lorenzo was still alive. We learn that, in addition to sharing Levi's goodness and bravery, Lorenzo also shared his depression. Soon after the war, Levi finds that Lorenzo has lost his love for life and is drinking to escape from it. Levi sees nothing irrational in this attitude; Lorenzo is "assured and coherent in his rejection of life."[143] Lorenzo dies of tuberculosis and alcoholism after living like a nomad, sleeping out in the open, but fiercely independent until the last, refusing all Levi's offers of help.

Levi ends this story with a chilling sentence: "He, who was not a survivor, had died of the survivors' disease."[144] In Lorenzo's case, the disease does not come from being enslaved or seeing family and friends murdered; it is not guilt for having survived when they fell; rather, it comes simply from seeing how evil life can be. Levi is not an ascetic: he does not make Lorenzo's goodness depend on his rejection of life. But "Lorenzo's Return" shows that for Levi, a man can be a paradigm of goodness even if he drowns in the end.

Levi had some vital needs that even Lorenzo, with his food and his goodness, could not fill. Levi craved conversation and culture, the opportunity to talk and think, to use his knowledge and reconnect with his heritage. In order to survive the Nazi assault on memory, to avoid becoming like Null Achtzehn, who had forgotten even his own name, Levi needed the chance to talk with a friend about something that transcended Auschwitz and the bestial struggle for survival.

In the chapter "Chemical Examination" of *If This Is a Man*, Levi recovers some of his identity in the process of passing the Nazis' exam to earn a job in the laboratory. He feels the old "fever of examinations, *my* fever of *my* examinations, that spontaneous mobilization of all my logical faculties and all my knowledge, which my friends at university so envied me."[145] While Alex the Kapo despises him for being the least manly of the applicants, when Levi is being tested by Pannwitz he feels himself growing in stature, as he succeeds in his violent effort to recall his memories of chemistry, as if trying to remember a previous incarnation.[146] But this reincarnation goes only so far; the chapter ends with Alex wiping his hand on Levi like a rag.

In the next chapter, "The Canto of Ulysses," Levi remembers literature instead of chemistry, and he does so with a friend instead of an enemy. His friend is Jean, a 24-year-old Alsatian student, the youngest prisoner in the chemical work squad, who has the job of "Pikolo," or assistant, to Alex. Jean is an exceptional Pikolo because, although he ingratiates himself with the Kapo and fights for his own survival, he does not neglect his less-privileged comrades.

One day at work, Jean does Levi a favor by choosing him to help fetch the soup pot from the kitchens. On their way to get it, the two of them are able to walk unencumbered. Jean cleverly chooses the longest possible path, so that they have a chance to talk. Appropriately, he is the first person in the book to call Levi by name. The appearance of "Primo" signals that this is the episode when Levi regains, or attains, his fullest identity thus far, becoming again a unique, cultured person and glimpsing the way he will make a name for himself—as a writer, a poet of the inferno.

If This Is a Man is also a story of a youth becoming a man, and so Levi and Jean discuss their mothers: "His mother too had scolded him for never knowing how much money he had in his pocket; his mother too would have been amazed if she had known that he had found his feet, that day by day he was finding his feet."[147] This is one of the only references to Levi's mother in all his writings, and it is only the word "too" that makes Jean's story his—shows him becoming a man, far from his mother's protective reach.

Levi offers to teach Jean some Italian, and Jean accepts (in fact, Jean also taught Levi German, but for this story Jean is more important as a listener, as Levi's first "reader"). Remarkably, Levi starts the lesson with the Canto of Ulysses from Dante's *Inferno*. He speaks six lines, translates, and then begins to pick his way through the rest of the Canto, quoting the lines he remembers and paraphrasing the rest. As they walk, another inmate named Levi, an engineer, waves to them. Primo Levi tells us that engineer Levi is a brave man who never loses his morale and never talks about eating. It is as if Levi has glimpsed a higher version of himself in this other Levi, who transcends the world of slavery and soup.

Then Levi reaches the climactic lines in which Ulysses exhorts his crew to brave the Atlantic and travel to the unpeopled realm beyond the sun:

> Consider what you came from: you are Greeks!
> You were not born to live like mindless brutes
> but to follow paths of excellence and knowledge.[148]

This speech, says Levi, is like the blast of a trumpet or the voice of God, making him forget who and where he is.[149] Jean begs him to repeat it because he sees that it does Levi good and because it speaks to him as well.

Levi continues translating but reaches a gap in his memory. He would give up his day's soup to fill it, but it is no use: the rest is silence.[150] They have reached the kitchen; time is running out. And so he skips forward to the end, in which Ulysses' ship is wrecked, "as pleased Another," i.e., God.

> I keep Pikolo back, it is vitally necessary and urgent that he listen, that he understand this "as pleased Another" before it is too late; tomorrow he or I might be dead, or we might never see each other again, I must tell him, I must explain to him . . . something gigantic that I myself have only just seen, in a flash of intuition, perhaps the reason for our fate, for our being here today. . . .[151]

The thought of Levi reciting the Canto of Ulysses in Auschwitz is so inspiring that it is easy to miss the darkness and complexity that accompany the illumination. Part of this complexity stems from the fact that Dante's Ulysses is quite different from Homer's Odysseus. Odysseus is the paradigmatic survivor, the brave, crafty man who survives not just the Trojan War but its aftermath: the ten-year journey in which he escapes cannibals, giants, witches, angry gods, and even a descent into Hell. Odysseus is the man who is saved, not drowned: first when Zeus wrecks his ship and kills all his sailors, next when Poseidon destroys his one-man boat and throws him into the sea, and finally when he lands safely on Ithaca with the Phaeacians, just before they are turned to stone. The *Odyssey* is about making it back home. We know Levi makes it back, since we are reading his book, and so we can rightly identify him with Odysseus: a man who goes through hell and emerges a hero, an exemplary man.

Dante's Ulysses suffers a completely different fate. In Homer's version, after Odysseus leaves Circe, his men butcher the sacred cattle of Helios and are punished with drowning by Zeus, but Odysseus survives and returns to Ithaca. In Dante's version, the fatal hubris belongs to Ulysses, not his men. After leaving Circe, he decides not to return to Ithaca after all, but to take his men on further adventures. As Ulysses explains it,

> Not sweetness of a son, not reverence
> for an aged father, not the debt of love
> I owed Penelope to make her happy,
>
> could quench deep in myself the burning wish
> to know the world and have experience
> of all man's vices, of all human worth.[152]

Ulysses' inspiring speech to his men, which strikes Levi like a trumpet blast, is undermined by these verses, in which we learn that he wants to experience all man's vices and that he is reneging on the duty he owes his family.

Even more depressingly, in Dante's version, Ulysses' quest is completely fruitless, perhaps suicidal. Having passed the pillars Hercules planted to warn men not to go any further, Ulysses sails for five months until he comes to a dark, endlessly tall mountain, which represents Purgatory. And then, the brief, brutal anticlimax:

> Our celebrations soon turned into grief:
> from the new land there rose a whirling wind
> that beat against the forepart of the ship

and whirled us round three times in churning waters;
the fourth blast raised the stern up high, and sent
the bow down deep, as pleased Another's will.[153]

That is the last we hear of the world's most famous adventurer. He doesn't reach the new world, the Blessed Isles, or even Ithaca; he fails to reach Purgatory and goes straight to Hell. He does not even stay in Limbo with Virgil and the other virtuous pagans; rather, he is sent down into the circle of the fraudulent counselors (all the more reason to distrust his exhortations to his sailors about knowledge and excellence).

Levi's narration reenacts this terrible anticlimax. Ulysses' speech rouses him, as it does Ulysses' men, to thoughts of grandeur, but just as he is about to explain his gigantic intuition to Jean, they reach the soup queue, and instead of the beautiful Italian of Dante, we hear the hellishly mundane German, French, and Polish words for cabbages and turnips. Then, bringing *The Inferno* and Auschwitz together in a terrifying image of drowning, Levi ends the chapter with Dante's line, "over our heads the hollow seas closed up."

Looking back, we realize that Levi has subtly presaged the anticlimax in earlier passages. The great speech by Ulysses strikes him like "the voice of God," but what does that mean, exactly, when we know that Levi does not believe in God? The speech makes him forget who he is and where he is, which suggests magical transcendence but also delusional escapism and a loss of identity. He has also prepared us for this turn in the previous chapter, "Chemical Examination," which follows an identical course: When his triumphant effort to remember his scientific knowledge ends, Levi feels dull and flat, watching

Pannwitz record his fate in incomprehensible symbols and then getting used as a rag by Alex.[154]

But Levi's anticlimactic ending does not mean that the search for human knowledge and excellence (virtue, in the classical sense) is nothing but a vain delusion, an express route to hell. Even in Dante, the thrill of Ulysses' magnificent speech transcends its pathos; all the more so in Levi, who lacks Dante's Christian reservations about the pagan adventurer. In fact, in an interview discussing this passage, Levi rather shockingly calls God's punishment of Ulysses the "punishment of a barbarian god for human daring" and links it to the barbaric Nazis' punishment of the Jews for their intellectual daring.[155] Levi's oral commentary is more radical and less ambiguous than the text itself, but, clearly, his sympathies are with Ulysses, not God.

While Levi sometimes refuses to link his survival to any virtue (saying it was the worst who survived), at other times he attributes his physical and moral survival to one particular virtue: not strength, bravery, piety, solidarity, or even goodness, but curiosity. He writes in *Moments of Reprieve* that his attentiveness to the people and the world around him was an important factor in his physical and spiritual salvation.[156] He told Philip Roth that the exceptional spiritedness with which he spent his year in the Lager resulted from his intense wish to understand, his constant curiosity.[157] For Levi, the urge to explore that leads Ulysses to his death is a cardinal virtue, not a sin.

Levi revisits this scene many years later in *The Drowned and the Saved* and affirms that his memories of the Canto were not in vain.

> Then and there they had great value. They made it possible for
> me to reestablish a link with the past, saving it from oblivion

and reinforcing my identity....They elevated me in my own
eyes and those of my interlocutor. They granted me a respite,
ephemeral but not hebetudinous, in fact liberating and differ-
entiating: in short, a way to find myself.[158]

Literature elevates, liberates, and differentiates. It allows a writer
to help others and transcend them at the same time. Literature
is a path to excellence and knowledge that has proved more
successful than Ulysses' voyage. And yet, the fate of Ulysses
remains a caution: the writer, too, may be tempted by hubris
and callousness, the dereliction of duty and the failure to care.

In "The Canto of Ulysses," Levi is not just recalling Dante
and Ulysses as models of humanity; he is also befriending
Jean the Pikolo. As they talk, listen, teach and help each other,
Levi and Jean enact, but also go beyond, the Ulyssean vision
of humanity as a pursuit of excellence and knowledge. Jean
wants to learn Italian. He has moved beyond the anti-language
of blows, the private languages of faith and discipline, and
even the national languages of friends and compatriots; he is
learning the language of an other. Jean succeeds where Ulysses
fails: he takes care of his less privileged comrades and helps
them survive. Ulysses tells his men they are not brutes, but
Greeks; Jean, implicitly, signals to Levi that he is not a brute,
but a man.

A subsequent chapter, "Kraus," reveals how Levi has been
changed by his experience with Jean. Again, Levi recounts a
work day. As Jean had been kind to him, he is kind to Kraus,
the inexperienced Hungarian. Like Jean, Levi surmounts a language barrier, making a long speech to Kraus in bad German,
but slowing, separating the words, making sure that Kraus
understands.[159] He tells Kraus his happy dream of the two

of them, warm and well-fed after the war, and Kraus cries tears of gratitude. Like "The Canto of Ulysses," "Kraus" ends in a terrible anticlimax. Levi tells the reader that the dream was invented (like Ulysses, he is a false counselor), and that Kraus is nothing to him: "nothing like everything is nothing down here, except the hunger inside and the cold and the rain around."[160] But again, the anti-climax does not annihilate the climax. Levi's story is false but good: a spark of humanity in the void.

For Levi, the complete man combines the goodness of Lorenzo with the greatness of Odysseus: he is capable of both self-sacrifice and self-discovery. In his own life, Levi emulated both men. He named both of his children, Lisa Lorenza and Renzo Cesare, after Lorenzo. He cared for others: instead of traveling, he remained in his family home to care for his aged mother for 40 years. At the same time, he pursued his epic voyage in search of excellence and knowledge through literature. For his epitaph, Levi once suggested the words Homer uses for Odysseus: *polla plankte*—"forever erring" or "driven to wander" (sadly, Levi's gravestone bears only his name, dates, and Auschwitz number).

As a prisoner at Auschwitz, it was not possible to be a true man: good like Lorenzo or great like Odysseus. But as soon as the Nazis fled, Levi got a chance and took it, as he describes in "The Story of Ten Days," the final chapter of *If This Is a Man*. He was sick with scarlet fever and staying with ten other patients in the infectious disease ward, including the two French Resistance fighters, Charles and Arthur, whom he befriended. The three of them scavenged for food, built a homemade stove, and tended to their sicker comrades. As Levi describes it, "Suddenly your neighbor was no longer your adversary in the struggle for life but a human being who was entitled to be helped."[161] Goodness had returned, as had culture: Levi found a French adventure novel, *Remorques*, about a brave tugboat skipper battling the raging elements, and he paused from his own fight for survival to read the whole book in one sitting.

In the next ward over, the patients were sicker and less organized. Of those patients, Levi helped only the two Italians. One terrible night, when the Russians bombed the camp and destroyed a nearby hut, some of the other patients, naked and wretched, begged for shelter in Levi's hut, but Levi and his friends barricaded them out.[162] An interview with Germaine Greer contains this fascinating exchange about a similar episode:

Greer: The episode...that I found the most appalling and morally ambiguous was when those of you hiding out in the scarlatina ward heard other patients in the next room groaning for water and ignored their pleading.

Levi: My subjective impression was very different. And still is today. I wrote to Charles, the Frenchman who was with me there, and we confessed to each other that those ten days were our "finest hour." Of course, we've censored and suppressed the fact that we didn't give water to everyone. However, we did try to save ten people's lives, and we succeeded, at least in part. We couldn't save four hundred, but perhaps we could save ten. And we did our best under the circumstances, even though we were both very sick. We remembered those ten days as our best time because we invented everything, the way to make the soup, the stove we made it on, the way to get water, even the medicines we needed. *We made our own world* [emphasis added]. There were hundreds around us who were not part of the world, but I think our calculation was the right one. It was better to try realistically to save ten than to succeed in saving no one.[163]

Levi acknowledges that human goodness and creativity are not perfect. Every inclusion implies an exclusion, and every creation implies an act of censorship and repression. But he is less appalled than Greer by the cost of virtue and more inclined to celebrate man's ability to make his own world.

Levi also made a beautiful comment on those days in his interview with Philip Roth:

In those memorable ten days, I truly did feel like Robinson Crusoe, but with one important difference. Crusoe set to work for his individual survival, whereas I and my two French companions were consciously and happily willing to work at last for a *just and human goal*, to save the lives of our sick comrades [emphasis added].[164]

Crusoe survives shipwreck and makes his own world; but Levi and his friends surpass him because the world they are making is good: it involves helping others. Levi makes an even more daring comparison in *If This Is a Man*: "We were broken by tiredness, but we seemed to have finally accomplished something useful, perhaps like God after the first day of Creation."[165]

Here, at last, is the man in Levi's humanist universe: a man so complete he feels like God. He is free, he has a goal, he helps others, he has friends to work with, and he uses his

virtue—his excellence and knowledge—to make his own
world. In a certain sense, Levi's bildungsroman feels finished
with this episode: he has become a man, and a fully human
man. He has found and made a world, a cosmos, and—in spite
of its lack of divinity and its inclusion of monstrous evil—
called it good.

But Levi is not just a character in this bildungsroman; he is also
the narrator and the author. He deepens his universe further
by reflecting on his role as the teller of this tale. Levi, so old-
fashioned in some respects, is distinctly modern in his empha-
sis on perspective and his complex self-awareness. Part of the
resonance of "The Story of Ten Days" stems from the fact that
the world-creating he does with Charles and Arthur is paral-
leled by his writing. Making a book, he creates a cosmos with
a just and human goal: to record faithfully acts of good and evil
and to help prevent the evil from recurring.

He knows that Auschwitz supplied him with his most
important subject matter and that, in a terrible irony, it was
the making of him as a man and a writer. He is like the Greek
soothsayer Tiresias, who, as Levi explains in his novel *The
Monkey's Wrench*, was abused and blinded by the gods, but
then, in compensation, given the ability to foresee the future, a
"strange power of speech."[166] As he often mentions, Levi is also
like Coleridge's Ancient Mariner, both condemned and privileged to tell a tale of shipwreck and devastation.

In *The Drowned and the Saved*, Levi discusses the motiva-
tions of those survivors, like him, who speak out about the
terror. Marshaling his authorities, he cites Dante, a Yiddish

saying, and the *Odyssey* on the pleasures of recounting one's sorrows. He explains that the imprisonment is the central event in the survivors' lives. Also, they wish to boast of their victories, differentiate themselves from others, and consolidate their identity as part of a special group. But most importantly, they were the witnesses to a crime of "planetary and epochal dimensions," and other people want their testimony.[167] As Levi writes,

> ...they speak, in fact (I can use the first person plural: I am not one of the taciturn) we speak also because we are invited to do so. Years ago, Norberto Bobbio wrote that the Nazi extermination camps were "not *one of the* events, but *the* monstrous, perhaps unrepeatable event of human history."[168]

Levi makes a bold claim: he was present at *the event*, the negative creation of our cosmos, and is thus uniquely qualified to interpret it. With deceptive humility (the word "I" appears only within parentheses), Levi says that he speaks because he is asked—which is true, but pales beside the larger truth that he speaks because he is weaving a new testament.

To be accurate—a good witness—Levi must convey the unique terror of the Lager and not assimilate it to other examples of evil and suffering. And yet, for his account to survive as literature (the only way it can, because no one reads old journalism) he must lend his account the ambiguous universality of literature. The reader must feel that she is reading about her own world and her own life, not something completely unrepeatable and alien. To solve this dilemma, Levi portrays the Lager as a new event that is nonetheless archetypal because it establishes a new reality. It is like the creation of the world, the handing down of the Ten Commandments, the birth of Jesus; it is a new and terrible Word, or number, inscribed on the flesh of its prophet.

In *If This Is a Man*, Levi calls the survivors' tales the "stories of a new Bible."[169] The new universe requires a new Moses, or requires each of us to be his own Moses. As a character in *If Not Now, When?* says, "If Moses was here with us...he wouldn't think twice about changing the laws. He'd smash the tablets...if he had seen the things we have."[170] Indeed, in *The Truce* Levi talks about a new Decalogue, or decalogue, claiming that it is "common knowledge that nobody is born with a decalogue already formed, but that everyone builds his own."[171] It is hardly common knowledge that everyone builds his own decalogue; to say so is to violate the most basic tenets of Judaism and Christianity. And yet, for all his boldness, Levi avoids hubris: he does not present a decalogue for us to adopt; rather, he says that each of us builds his own, "on the basis of his own experiences."[172] Levi can influence us, then, only if reading his book becomes a participatory experience, one we claim as our own.

One of the many mysteries of "The Canto of Ulysses" is the "something gigantic" that Levi saw, "perhaps the reason for our fate, for our being here today." It is odd that Levi never explains what it was. He leads us to expect a great theodicy like Dante's: a justification for all the evil and suffering. And yet Levi rejects all theodicies: as he says in *The Drowned and the Saved*, the experience of Auschwitz prevents him from conceiving any form of providence or transcendent justice.[173] But if it was a false revelation that Levi saw, we might expect him to tell us what it was, rather than leave it unspoken.

Perhaps then, Levi's revelation was true, but involved a truth that should not be spelled out. Perhaps while reciting Dante (or later, while writing "The Canto of Ulysses"), he intuited his role in the universe. He saw that he would live to tell the tale, like Homer's Odysseus or Dante's Pilgrim. He would not be one of the drowned, the anonymous mass; far from it. He would make a name for himself as a writer. But because this revelation is personal, self-oriented, and highly ambitious, Levi does not express it openly; he leaves it mysterious.

In *The Drowned and the Saved,* Levi calls the Lager, and having written about the Lager, "an important adventure that has profoundly modified me, given me maturity and a reason for life."[174] In his notes to the theatrical version of *If This Is a Man,* Levi compares himself to Odysseus telling his tale and says that many survivors hoped not to live *and* tell their story, but to live *in order to* tell their story.[175] Apparently, Levi did glimpse his future as a writer while still in the Lager. He began to compose the poem "Shemà" in his head and wrote prose in a notebook while working in the Nazi laboratory.[176] He destroyed these scraps for safety, but they were, perhaps, the first intimations of *If This Is a Man.*

The role of the writer gave Levi a reason for living, but it certainly did not dissolve his difficulties. In his preface to *Moments of Reprieve,* Levi describes himself as besieged by ghosts, begging him to help them survive as literary characters.[177] He is like Odysseus, who, on his descent to the underworld, finds himself mobbed by spirits, until he has to pull his sword and force them to speak one at a time. Levi only hints at the irony of having to make a selection of those who will survive, but the tragic echoes resound.

In telling their stories, Levi has to judge his fellow men: to view them with a gaze that might itself be inhuman. As he writes in *The Drowned and the Saved*:

> ...from my trade I contracted a habit that can be variously judged and defined at will as human or inhuman—the habit of never remaining indifferent to the individuals that chance brings before me. They are human beings but also "samples," specimens in a sealed envelope to be identified, analyzed, and weighed. Now, the sample book that Auschwitz had placed open before me was rich, varied, and strange, made up of friends, neutrals and enemies, yet in any case food for my curiosity, which some people, then and later, have judged to be detached.... [I]t should not seem cynical to say this, for me, as for...many other "fortunate" survivors, the Lager was a university. It taught us to look around and measure men.[178]

Much of Levi's education, like Dante's, is learning to tell good from evil, whom to pity and whom to condemn. As he notes in the essay "The Struggle for Life," while it is humiliating and debilitating to be perpetually judged, it is unnatural and dangerous to expect to avoid all judgment.[179] Every single human encounter involves a judgment delivered or received. Thus, Levi argues in the essay, parents should expect schools to judge their children, not to immunize them from judgment. Interestingly, Levi links this constant judgment to man's animal instinct to compete for life. Judgment is brutally agonistic, yet a necessary part of human goodness.

The great teller of tales, no matter how much he acknowledges his frailty and partiality, must command respect. In both his life and work, Levi deftly combined humility with strength. As his friend Charles from the "The Story of Ten Days" later described him: "such a modest man, almost self-effacing, yet able to display real authority."[180] To be authoritative one must surpass others. Thus, Levi entered into polemics with other Auschwitz authors, such as Jean Améry, and felt competitive about even good friends who wrote Auschwitz books, like Luciana Nissim and Bruno Vasari.[181] In addition to competing with friends and fellow travelers, Levi could be antagonistic toward great writers he considered overrated, including Proust ("boring"), Borges ("alien and distant"), and Dostoevsky ("wearisome").[182]

Even within *If This Is a Man*, Levi does not allow other characters to become tellers of tales and sometimes seems to envy or to understate their fluency. Perhaps this is a small part of the reason that Lorenzo is the great hero of the book: because he, a morose man who does his good deeds in silence, does not threaten Levi's role as storyteller. Perhaps this is why Levi never mentions that Alberto helped save him at the first selection with his better command of German. Perhaps it accounts for the fact that Jean the Pikolo is portrayed as the ideal listener, the student of Italian, and never as Levi's German teacher.

To be a storyteller is to be the maker of one's own destiny, a status that contradicts the basic thesis of *If This Is a Man*: that the Germans succeeded in turning all the inmates into bestial slaves. Later, in the *Moments of Reprieve* stories, Levi feels freer to offer exceptions, and we get to know other prisoners as creators of their own art. Rappoport delivers his "testament," Eddy performs his juggling act, Tischler tells his strange legend of Lilith, Ezra the cantor explains Yom Kippur to the Kapo, and Wolf plays a violin so ecstatically that even Elias the dwarf seems to see a vision of a better world. Levi is willing to serve as their scribe, as he does literally in the story "The Gypsy," in which he helps the illiterate Grigo compose a letter to his fiancée. In these stories, the inmates enter into real conversations with Levi; Tischler even argues with him about the creation of mankind. But in *If This Is a Man*, there can be only one storyteller.

But if Levi is authoritative, he is never authoritarian. Relentlessly, he urges us to doubt his word. As he cautions in *The Drowned and the Saved*, the recollections of survivors should be read with a critical eye because "memory is a marvelous but fallacious instrument."[183] Lest we be tempted to exempt Levi from his own rule, he tells us even more explicitly:

> This very book is drenched in memory; what's more, a distant memory. Thus it draws from a suspect source and must be protected against itself.[184]

The reader has an active role to play in protecting the book from itself, preventing it from hardening into dogma. In constantly comparing himself to Odysseus, Levi also reminds us that the better the storyteller, the better the liar. Odysseus is the master of both types of "plots": narratives and deceptions.[185] That is why Dante assigned him to a circle deep in Hell: the realm of the false counselors.

Levi weaves a cosmos, a literary work to be read alongside Homer and Dante, out of monstrous evils that real people committed and real people suffered—materials that would seem to enjoin scrupulous accuracy and fidelity. No wonder then that he often portrays himself not as a literary lion but as an

ordinary chemist who is forced to become a "writer-witness."
No wonder that, as he later admits about *If This Is a Man*,

> ...in those forty years I've constructed a sort of legend around
> that book, that I wrote it without a plan, that I wrote it on
> impulse, that I wrote it without reflecting at all....In fact, writ-
> ing is never spontaneous. Now that I think about it, I can see
> that this book is full of literature, literature absorbed through
> the skin, even while I was rejecting it (because I was a bad stu-
> dent of Italian literature).[186]

No wonder he ascribes his way of looking at the "sample book"
of Auschwitz not to his gifts and needs as a writer but to his
training as a chemist.[187] No wonder he characterizes the language of *If This Is a Man* as "inhuman" and that of *The Truce* as
"anti-human."[188] Dante could defend himself from the charge
of building a literary edifice out of hellish sufferings by point-
ing out that it was a poem, not a chronicle, and that he was
a humble penitent showing others, as he had been shown by
Beatrice and Virgil, the path to God. Levi lacks those defenses:
he has to stand by the accuracy of his words and yet caution
us against them.

Levi knows the danger of hubris: even a hero like Ulysses
can get shipwrecked. And books drown, too: *If This Is a Man*
itself nearly drowned. All the major publishers rejected it; a
minor publisher printed 2,500 copies and folded. Six hundred unsold copies, stored in a remainder warehouse in
Florence, were, Levi writes, literally drowned in an autumn
flood.[189] Only after ten years of apparent death did the book
come back to life, when it was republished in 1957.[190] And
so, in his writing, Levi remains circumspect. He does not

explain the "something gigantic." He does not exhort us like Ulysses telling his sailors that they are men. Instead, he patiently asks whether we are men, and whether he himself is a man, until his questioning becomes not an epic but an epochal tale.

Six

TRUCES

AFTER THE LIBERATION of Auschwitz, Levi found that his trials were not over, his moral and psychological growth was not finished, and his cosmos was incomplete. He was rescued in January 1945 by the Russians, who took him first to a refugee camp in Katowice, Poland, and then to another in Starye Dorogi, Russia. It would be a full nine months before he made it back home to Turin, and those nine months in limbo—an odd time, pregnant with both desolation and gaiety—became the next major stage in his development: a stage he describes in his second book, *The Truce* (published in the United States as *The Reawakening*).

At the opening of *If This Is a Man*, Levi portrays himself as "twenty-four, with little wisdom, no experience, and a decided tendency...to live in an unrealistic world of my own, a world inhabited by civilized Cartesian phantoms...."[1] By contrast, here is how he describes himself three months after leaving Auschwitz, in his first letter home to his family:

> Maybe I'll come home shoeless, but in compensation for my ragged state I've learned German and a bit of Russian and Polish, I also know how to get out of many situations without losing my nerve, and how to withstand moral and physical suffering. To economise on the barber I'm sporting a beard. I know how to make a cauliflower or turnip soup, cook potatoes in a hundred different ways (all without seasoning). I know, too, how to assemble, light, and clean stoves. And I've been through an incredible variety of careers: assistant bricklayer, navvy, sweep, porter, grave-digger, interpreter, cyclist, tailor, thief, nurse, fence, stone-breaker. I've even been a chemist![2]

Levi uses this jaunty, picaresque tone, so different from that of *If This Is a Man*, throughout *The Truce*, but he weaves it together with sober, haunted reflections on the aftermath of the war and the Lager.

In some ways, Levi presents the world of *The Truce* as the opposite of the world of *If This Is a Man*: peace instead of war, wild freedom instead of brutal confinement, anarchy instead of totalitarianism, disorderly Russians instead of rule-obsessed Germans, wandering instead of confinement, comedy instead of tragedy. It is, as Levi says of one of the refugee camps, "the Lager upside down."[3] And yet, as Levi is quick to explain, this new world is not the Promised Land. The inmates' hope for an upright and just world, miraculously reestablished, was naïve and based on too-sharp distinctions between past and future, good and evil. Emerging from the inferno, they find themselves not in paradise, but on a pitiless deserted plain.[4] It is a "primeval Chaos...swarming with scalene, defective, abnormal human specimens."[5] And alongside these strange presences are terrible absences as well. Of the 489 Jews on Levi's transport to Auschwitz, only 24 returned alive.[6]

Structurally, the world of *The Truce* is quite continuous with the world of *If This Is a Man*. The bulk of the narrative takes place in camps: first Auschwitz, then the refugee camps. The book is roughly chronological, divided, just like *If This is a Man*, into seventeen short chapters. Once again, Levi concentrates not on plot or history but on the different characters he encounters, offering brief, penetrating sketches of their personalities and their basic attitudes toward life—continuing his research into what it means to be a man. But as we get to know these characters, we find that the new, postwar universe is radically different. If Levi's model in *If This Is a Man* is the *Inferno*, his model in *The Truce* is the *Odyssey*: an epic not about hell but about earth, with all its hellish and heavenly aspects.

One of the surprises of *The Truce* is the somewhat rosy view Levi offers of the Russians, particularly since he wrote the book in the early 1960s, when the horrors of Stalinism, and its many points of resemblance to Nazism, were well known. In all of Levi's writing, it is the only time that he seems slightly sentimental and naïve. Some of the reasons are doubtless personal: after all, the Russians defeated the Nazis, rescued Levi from Auschwitz, fed and took care of him, and returned him safely to Turin. Other reasons are purely literary: it makes *The Truce* a better story to have the Russians be heroic and comic, rather than tragic, and to have them offer constant points of comparison and difference to the Germans.

The Russians are important to Levi for their earthiness, their physical vitality, and their exuberance. Their physicality has a strongly metaphysical import, as we see at the beginning of *The Truce,* when the first four Russian soldiers on horseback arrive at Auschwitz:

> It seemed to us, and so it was, that the nothing full of death in which we had wandered like spent stars for ten days had found its own solid center, a nucleus of condensation: four men, armed, but not against us: four messengers of peace, with rough and boyish faces beneath their heavy fur hats.[7]

They are the Four Horsemen, not of the Apocalypse but of a reverse Apocalypse, a new beginning. Out of the black hole of Auschwitz, the "nothing full of death," the "spent stars," comes a cosmic rebirth.

Levi receives his baptism into this new universe when the Russians make him bathe. The Russian bath is not like the humiliating, "black-mass" bath the Germans required upon entry into Auschwitz, nor is it like the functional, antiseptic, automated bath the Americans would later require. The Russian bath is "to human measure, extemporaneous and crude."[8] Levi prefers the Russian bath, but makes clear, as he did when bathing with Steinlauf in *If This Is a Man,* that he rejects being "baptized" into anyone else's order, no matter how appealing. He describes it as an attempt to "strip us of the vestiges of our former life, to make us new men consistent with their own models, to impose their brand on us."[9]

But the word "brand," with its tragic echoes of the Nazi tattoos, is as close as Levi comes to invoking the totalitarianism of the Soviet regime. For him, the Russians' version of communism at the refugee camp at Katowice is primitive and idyllic, not Stalinist. The whole group lives in harmony, without a timetable or regulations but with friendly simplicity, like a large family.[10] Levi uses comedy to show both affection and mild derision for the Soviets. A typical stock figure is the huge Mongolian who serves as a guard. When it gets cold, the guard simply deserts his post to drink vodka with the refugees, or gives his sten gun to one of them to replace him while he dozes by the stove.

At times in *The Truce*, the Russians function more like noble savages than like emissaries from the land of Tolstoy, Dostoevsky, Lenin, and Stalin. Levi's patronizing idealization of them falls flat when it is earnest—when he talks about "those rough and open faces, the good soldiers of the Red Army, the valiant men of the old and new Russia, gentle in peace and fierce in war."[11] Much funnier, and more characteristic, is the episode in which the Italian refugees stage a play called *The Shipwreck of the Spiritless* (a title too Levian to be true), in which the Italians are allegorized as castaways and the Russians as cannibals, naked and tattooed, prattling in a primitive and unintelligible jargon.[12] Amazingly, the Russians tolerate this performance, whether through incomprehension or good humor, and, that very night, they wake up the refugees—not to send them to Siberia, as the refugees fear, but rather, inexplicably, to pay them all "salaries."

In a similar episode, the Russians turn a blind eye when the refugees begin stealing horses and killing them for food. When they finally lock up one refugee for setting up a butcher shop, their chaotic administrative style results in the butcher's being given three rations a day instead of one, so that he returns from his ten days of punishment as fat as a pig and full of joie de vivre.[13] The anarchic lawlessness of the Russians is very different from the totalitarian lawlessness of the Lager. Rather, it resembles the Italians' cheerful disregard for rules, which Levi believes helped save Jews from the Nazis. As Chaim, a character in *If Not Now, When?*, explains, Italians make a game out of disobeying laws. They know the Ten Commandments by heart but they follow two or three at most. Because they are naturally subversive, they delight in evading Mussolini and Hitler's laws against the Jews.[14]

Given the contrast between the Russian camp and the Nazi camp that Levi had survived, it is not hard to see why he might idealize the Soviet Union as harboring "gigantic vigour, a Homeric capacity for joy and abandon, a primordial vitality, an uncontaminated pagan appetite for carousals, carnivals, massive revelry."[15] The Russians are a vehicle through which Levi can explore a joyful love of life and humanity—something very much a part of Levi's universe but impossible to render fully in *If This Is a Man*.

Levi makes the Russians like characters in books by his favorite author, François Rabelais. Introducing Rabelais in *The Search for Roots*, Levi praises him for revealing the joys of gluttony, drinking bouts, and debauchery, and for teaching us that "[T]o love human beings means to love them as they are, body and soul, warts and all."[16] In another essay, "François Rabelais," Levi elaborates on the links between joy, love, and virtue:

> Gigantic above every other thing is Rabelais' and his creatures' capacity for joy. This boundless and luxuriating epic of satisfied flesh unexpectedly reaches heaven by another route: because

the man who feels joy is like the man who feels love, he is
good, he is grateful to his Creator for having created him, and
therefore he will be saved.[17]

Although Levi does not believe in a Creator, he is obsessed
with salvation. In a graph he draws to accompany *The Search
for Roots*, Levi traces two paths of salvation, one through understanding and one through laughter. To salvage life, we must
laugh and love it, "warts and all."

If Levi did not become as life-affirming as Rabelais, it was not
just because he had suffered so much evil and death. It was also
because, even as he rediscovered his joie de vivre, he remained
ambivalent about earthly appetites, especially sexual ones. As
one of his female friends commented, "All his life Primo was
terrified of us women."[18]

In the second chapter of *The Truce*, Levi offers contrasting
portraits of three characters living in Auschwitz after the liberation: Noah, Jadzia, and Frau Vita. Noah is the Minister of
the Latrines, but Levi says that there is nothing sordid about
him, or, if there is, it is canceled out by his vitality, the way he
rejoices in the air he breathes and the earth on which he walks.
Levi compares Noah to Rabelais's giant, Pantagruel, and writes
him this ambiguous paean:

> ...Noah, a high-flying bird, cruised along all the roads of the
> camp from dawn to dusk, on the seat of his repugnant cart,
> cracking his whip and singing at the top of his voice; the cart
> stopped before the entrance of each Block, and while his troop,

filthy and stinking, hurried, cursing, through their repulsive
task, Noah wandered around the feminine dormitories like an
oriental prince, dressed in an arabesque many-colored coat, full
of patches and braid. His encounters were like so many hurri-
canes. He was the friend of all men and the lover of all women.
The deluge was over; in the black sky of Auschwitz, Noah saw a
rainbow shine out, and the world was his, to repopulate.[19]

Something in Levi wants to overcome his virginal horror of
sexuality, his sense of it as dirty and excremental; he wants the
sordidness canceled out by the vital energy. But another part
of him remains repulsed by the bestial Noah, with his "filthy
and stinking" troop.

If Levi's sexual horror is somewhat muted in his reactions
to men, it comes to the forefront in his reactions to women.
Jadzia, the promiscuous Polish girl, has stupefied eyes; she is
at once passive and overwhelming: "if the man waited for her,
Jadzia wrapped herself around him, incorporated him, took
possession of him, with the blind, mute, tremulous, slow, but
sure movements which amoebae show under the microscope."
If Noah's animality is described with the somewhat appealing
images of horse and a bird, Jadzia is a mollusk "throwing out
her tenuous threads."[20]

Levi contrasts both Noah and Jadzia with another character in liberated Auschwitz, Frau Vita. Unlike those sexual
creatures, Frau Vita bears all humans a love simple and frater-
nal.[21] She is the only person who bothers with the invalids and
children, and, when she has free time after that, she spends
it frenetically washing the floors and windows, as if trying
to wash herself and the world clean of the Lager's evil. Levi
finds her chaste goodness, as he finds his own, both admirable

and pathetic: after completing her furious washing, Frau Vita comes back exhausted and sits panting on Levi's bunk, tearful, starved of words and intimacy. In the evenings, unable to bear the solitude, she sings and dances by herself, clasping an imaginary man to her breast.[22] Like Levi, she embraces only nonexistent partners, thus maintaining—intentionally or not—her purity.

Later in *The Truce,* Levi describes four people who choose to live in the woods outside the refugee camp at Starye Dorogi. Two of them are German prostitutes, who, even more than Jadzia, represent the bestial, vicious side of nature. But in contrast to them, Levi offers us Cantarella, a former sailor who has reverted to primitivism, not like a beast, but like a religious hermit. Although he lives alone in a hut made from branches, dressed only in a loincloth, Levi describes him as a "contemplative."[23] Cantarella makes pots and pans out of war scrap and gives them to refugee couples who have decided to "get married" and set up house together. He does this "priestly activity," Levi writes, with "great skill and religious diligence."[24]

Velletrano, another Italian refugee, also finds his identity as a savage outside the camp. He lives in the forest, barefoot and naked, trapping animals, sleeping on the dirt, and inviting everybody to "Homeric feasts" of roasted meat.[25] In contrast to the bestial victims in Levi's portrayal of Auschwitz, wild Velletrano exemplifies the essential unity—rather than the terrible fragility—of man. As in *If This Is a Man*, Levi evokes Ulysses' great speech about men being made to pursue virtue and knowledge, but this time in a comic mode, describing Velletrano in these words: "as he was still born of man, in his own way he pursued virtue and knowledge, and day by day perfected his art and instruments; he fabricated a knife, then a spear and an axe, and had he had time, without doubt he would have rediscovered agriculture and pasturage."[26] At Auschwitz, even the most civilized men lost their humanity; here in the Russian woods, even the wildest men can find it.

If This Is a Man is a book about man's capacity for good and evil; its hero is Lorenzo, the bricklayer, the good man. *The Truce* is about man's capacity for life, and its hero is Cesare, the trader, the Odyssean man, the deceiver and adventurer, who is saved by Levi in the infirmary of Auschwitz and, in return, gives him back his *Lebenslust*. A key question of *The Truce* is whether it is possible to love life after Auschwitz, and Cesare's answer is "yes." In Cesare, Levi creates a character wild and anarchic, yet somehow deeply civilized; lustful and promiscuous, yet somehow never bestial.

The real-life model for Cesare, a man named Lello Perugia, was much less of a ragamuffin trickster: he was a Communist accountant, not a former street vendor. But Levi's theme required a more Rabelaisian figure than reality had supplied. Interestingly, he rebaptizes Lello with his own father's name, Cesare, as if to do belated justice to his father's embrace of life and all its pleasures: his old commandment to drink, smoke, and go with girls.

Just as in Auschwitz, where Levi was Alberto's trading assistant, so in *The Truce* he becomes Cesare's trading assistant—this time not for survival, but for joy. Levi writes that watching Cesare's enterprises reconciles him to the world and relights the joy of living that Auschwitz had extinguished.[27] Even in Levi's comic mode, the stakes are high, and the vocabulary is ethical: "a virtue like Cesare's is good in itself, in an absolute sense; it is enough to confer nobility on a man, to redeem his many other defects, to save his soul."[28]

Cesare, for all his moral lapses, has a charisma, a super-abundance of life, that justifies him. In one of his typical adventures, he, Levi, and some others are camping out in the woods en route to Starye Dorogi, and as they start to prepare their rations of kasha and peas, Cesare says, "To hell with your dinner!" He announces that they are going to have a party, with a roast chicken, and he takes Levi off in the darkness, in the middle of the Pripet marshes, lacking money and speaking no Russian, to find and trade for a chicken.[29] As a result, they get not only a chicken but also an adventure; they get a surplus of experience, not just what was rationed out to them.

Levi is delighted to observe Cesare fobbing off a brass ring as gold or injecting chickens with water to make them seem plumper. Commerce remains, as it was at Auschwitz, a zero-sum game: at the market, even Cesare's "virtue" harms the buyers, because it charms them, and in the "hard laws of commerce what is of advantage to the seller is of disadvantage to the purchaser."[30] But now a zero-sum game can be a "live and fortifying spectacle."[31] Cesare is not like Dante's Ulysses, sent to hell for being a fraudulent counselor; rather, he is like Homer's Odysseus, praised by the heavenly goddess Athena for being, like her, the best at deceptions.

One indicator of Cesare's special place in Levi's universe is the fact that Levi allows him to speak for himself, with many lines of dialogue—a distinction no other character in *The Truce* or *If This Is a Man* can claim. Cesare's distinctive way of speaking, and the fact that Levi takes the trouble to re-create (or create) it, showcases his individuality, autonomy, and vitality. Levi invents many memorable characters, but apart from the character Primo Levi he does not usually endow them with the sustained, mysterious autonomy of an Ivan Karamazov or a Sancho Panza. Cesare is the exception. Although based on a real person, he is very much a novelistic character; he seems to live and breathe on his own, independent of his creator.

Another indicator of Cesare's special relationship with Levi is a scene in which Cesare pretends to be Levi in order to exit the refugee camp at Katowice for the day (for some reason, Levi has permission, but Cesare does not). Levi gives his identity card to the guard, who dutifully checks it and lets him pass; Levi then passes the card through the barbed wire to Cesare, who also presents it to the guard. The guard asks his name, he says "Primo Levi," the name matches the card, and out Cesare goes. In the comical world of *The Truce,* Levi's name, which was such a precious, inalienable thing in *If This Is a Man,* is now available to be shared with his friend.[32]

Levi also allows Cesare to nickname—or "baptize"—him "Lapè," meaning "rabbit" or "rabbit skin," because of the way Levi's hair comes back smooth and silky after having been cropped.[33] Being compared to an animal was dehumanizing in *If This Is a Man,* but here, it is comical and affectionate. His acceptance of the nickname is all the more surprising because, as we have seen, Levi is repulsed by rabbits and associates them with men who are humiliated and outcast, knowing only food and sex.[34] Cesare, of course, is in love with food and sex, and some of his love has rubbed off on Levi.

But Cesare is not the only trader in *The Truce*. Almost equally important is Mordo Nahum—or, as Levi usually calls him, to make him a more representative figure, "the Greek." During his imprisonment, Levi had become fascinated by the Greek Jews of Salonica, who dominated the black market of Auschwitz. As he writes in *If This is a Man*, they were

> ...the repositories of a concrete, mundane, conscious wisdom, in which the traditions of all the Mediterranean civilizations blend together. That this wisdom was transformed in the camp into the systematic and scientific practice of theft and sei- zure of positions and the monopoly of the bargaining Market, should not let one forget that their aversion to gratuitous bru- tality, their amazing consciousness of the survival of at least a potential human dignity made of the Greeks the most coherent national nucleus in the Lager, and in this respect, the most civilized.[35]

Levi first meets Mordo Nahum en route from Auschwitz to Katowice. Once again, Levi is entranced by a more worldly companion and becomes his assistant and foil as they set out "in the problematical search for human kind."[36] Like Levi, when work is done, the Greek tells stories with warmth and an unsuspected humanity and likes to talk about the meaning of knowledge, justice, spirit, and truth.[37]

The Greek has managed to get himself a fine new pair of shoes, and he pours scorn on Levi for wearing shoes that fall apart. Levi is impressed by the Greek's concrete wisdom, writ- ing that the Greek is a rogue, but with a moral code.[38] But Levi

also calls the Greek a wise serpent, evoking cynicism and amo-
rality.[39] In another discourse on shoes, the Greek explains that,
when war is raging, you have to get shoes even before you get
food in order to survive.

> "But the war is over," I objected: and I thought it was over, as
> did many in those months of truce, in a much more universal
> sense than one dares to think today. "There is always war,"
> replied Mordo Nahum memorably.[40]

Both men had been in the Lager, but while Levi feels it as a terrible anomaly, the Greek considers it just another chapter in an
old story: man is a wolf to man.

For the Greek, trade is war by other means. His brutality is
exposed when he reappears later in the narrative as a pimp,
lording it over a field full of prostitutes. Levi recalls how the
Greek had once exclaimed, angrily, "Tell me an article I have
never dealt in!"[41] Women, it turns out, are mere articles of commerce to him. The Greek, in some ways so similar to Cesare, is
also his opposite:

> Cesare was full of human warmth, always, at every moment
> of his life, not just outside office hours like Mordo Nahum.
> For Cesare, "work" was sometimes an unpleasant necessity, at
> other times an amusing opportunity to meet people, and not a
> frigid obsession, or a luciferesque affirmation of himself. One
> of them was free, the other was a slave to himself; one was
> miserly and reasonable, the other prodigal and fantastic. The
> Greek was a lone wolf, in an eternal war against all, old before
> his time, closed in the circle of his own joyless pride; Cesare
> was a child of the sun, everybody's friend; he knew no hatred
> or contempt, was as changeable as the sky, joyous, cunning

and ingenuous, bold and cautious, very ignorant, very innocent and very civilized.[42]

As we compare the Greek and Cesare, we realize what fine distinctions Levi draws between people, like Dante assigning them
to the multitudinous strata of hell, purgatory, and heaven. In
addition to new types of vice, we learn about another of Levi's
cardinal virtues: human warmth, a love of life and humanity
that makes Cesare "everybody's friend," despite his sometimes
unethical behavior.

Levi works an even more complex reversal of *If This Is a Man*
in his depiction of the Carabiniere, an Italian soldier who ends
up with the refugees on a train back to Italy (the Carabinieri
were a unit of the Italian army). Ironically, Levi describes this
Fascist soldier as playing a role that would normally belong to
a Jew in an anti-Semitic story, calling him a predestined victim who inspires contempt, mockery, and malignant gossip.
He is a scapegoat on whom the others, as if by a mysterious
agreement, unload their bad tempers and their desire to hurt.
Like a stereotypical Jew, he suffers acutely but passively from
the persecution: he is polite, mild, touchy, and sensitive.[43] Levi
emulates the process of stereotyping by referring to him only
as "the Carabiniere." He tells us that grotesque legends circu-
late about the Carabinieri—that they take an oath to kill their
fathers and mothers.

The Carabiniere bears his pain in silence. But, in contrast to
the victims of *If This Is a Man*, the Carabiniere does not drown
in his silence; instead, he is saved by a *deus ex machina*: the

sudden, mysterious appearance of a youth named Pista. Pista speaks only Hungarian, and no one can understand him. In the Lager such incommunicability would have meant certain death, but in this new world it becomes a source of joy. Pista sings beautiful Hungarian songs and tries, unsuccessfully, to explain them, with gestures that make everyone laugh. Pista befriends the lonely Carabiniere—he is as fond of him as a brother—and this mysterious camaraderie, crossing all lines, slowly cleanses the Carabiniere of his "original sin."[44] True, the other refugees think, "the Carabiniere had killed his father and mother, but, all told, he must be a good boy, since Pista followed him."[45] Italian Fascists like the Carabiniere had captured Levi and delivered him to the Nazis two years earlier, but he shows no inclination for revenge. Instead, he uses the Carabiniere to dramatize a comic process of reintegration and overcoming, a perfect reversal of the Nazi assault on the Jews.

As *The Truce* draws to a close, Levi makes it clear that while many small reversals of Auschwitz are possible, no complete erasure can ever take place. The new world belongs to Cesare, but also to the Greek; the possibility of man being a wolf to man is always present. Levi's title, *La tregua*, is illuminating. "Tregua," in addition to "truce," means "cease-fire, break, or respite"— moments of reprieve shorter than those offered by a truce. Levi explains the title toward the end of the book, as he and his friend Leonardo are riding the train back into Italy. While the other refugees celebrate, he and Leonardo remain lost in silence.

[W]e knew that on the thresholds of our homes, for good or ill, a trial awaited us, and we anticipated it with fear. We felt in our veins the poison of Auschwitz.... Soon, tomorrow, we should have to give battle, against enemies still unknown, outside ourselves and inside; with what weapons, what energies, what willpower?... [W]e felt emptied and defenseless. The months just past, although hard, of wandering on the margins of civilization now seemed to us like a truce, a parenthesis of unlimited availability, a providential but unrepeatable gift of fate.[46]

Odysseus faces a trial—a bloody battle with the suitors—when he returns home, but his world has remained sane and comprehensible to him, and he does not feel poisoned by the carnage he has endured and wreaked in the intervening twenty years. Levi's two years have made him feel in many ways like a man, richly endowed and capable, and yet at the same time they have left him "emptied and defenseless."

At the beginning and ending of *The Truce* are two passages that enclose it like matching parentheses, one in poetry and one in prose. The opening poem is "Reveille," which centers on the Polish word *Wstawàch* ("get up"), which served as the brutal wake-up call at Auschwitz. Levi recalls how after a night in which the inmates dreamed of going home, eating, and telling their story, the dreaded call, *Wstawàch*, would crack the heart in the breast. Now, the refugees have found their homes, satisfied their hunger, and told their stories. But instead of fulfillment, they find, in the end, a renewal of terror:

> It is time. Soon we shall hear again
> The alien command:
>   *Wstawàch.*

The Truce closes with two intricate paragraphs that interrelate in complicated ways with "Reveille." Surprisingly, Levi allots only one paragraph to his return to Turin and tells us almost nothing about his reunion with his family and friends: only that they were alive and not expecting him. What makes him happiest, apparently, is the "liberating joy" of recounting his story, but even that joy is destroyed in the final paragraph, when Levi describes a nightmare that still visits him. In the dream, he is sitting peacefully at a table with family, friends, or work colleagues, when he begins to feel the deep and subtle anguish of an impending threat. Then everything collapses:

> Now everything has changed to chaos; I am alone in the center of a grey and turbid nothing, and now, I *know* what this means, and I also know that I have always known it; I am in the Lager once more, and nothing is true outside the Lager. All the rest was a brief pause, a deception of the senses, a dream; my family, nature in flower, my home. Now this inner dream, this dream of peace, is over, and in the outer dream, which continues, gelid, a well-known voice resounds: a single word, not imperious, but brief and subdued. It is the dawn command of Auschwitz, a foreign word, feared and expected: get up, "*Wstawàch*."[47]

The chapter is called "The Awakening," which carries two contradictory meanings. It signifies the return from the nightmare of Auschwitz to normal life, but also the reveille that calls one from a dream of normal life back to Auschwitz: the alien word that ends the opening poem and the book: *Wstawàch*.

Levi had dreamed of reaching the ultimate reality of things, but now he finds himself in a reality that is fundamentally unstable, shifting back and forth between home and Lager, so that it is impossible to tell which is a dream and which is real.

It is not a new Jerusalem; it is merely a fragile truce. Not only the adventure tale of Levi's journey, his "unrepeatable gift," but also daily life itself can seem merely an oasis within the boundless chaos of the Lager.[48] The Lager is not just a bad memory, a source of specific pain and shame. It is cosmic, as Levi writes in *The Drowned and the Saved*:

> ...[E]veryone suffered from an unceasing discomfort that polluted sleep and was nameless...an atavistic anguish whose echo one hears in the second verse of Genesis: the anguish inscribed in everyone...of a deserted and empty universe crushed under the spirit of God but from which the spirit of man is absent: not yet born or already extinguished.[49]

Even beyond the survivors' shame, Levi sees another, vaster shame: the shame of the world.[50] During the war, the majority of Germans turned themselves into islands through willed ignorance. But their victims could not be islands, even if they wanted to:

> The ocean of pain, past and present, surrounded us, and its level rose from year to year until it almost submerged us....It was not possible for us nor did we want to become islands; the just among us...felt remorse, shame, and pain for the misdeeds that others and not they had committed, and in which they felt involved, because they sensed that what had happened around them in their presence, and in them, was irrevocable. Never again could it be cleansed; it would prove that man, the human species—we, in short—had the potential to construct an infinite enormity of pain....[51]

In place of the universal peace for which he had hoped, Levi finds an anguish that is universal in two senses: first, in the sense of the primal chaos of a world without God, and second, in the sense of Nazi damage to the human spirit that can never be undone.

The truce is a metaphor that concentrates many levels of Levi's thought. In autobiographical terms, it refers to the parenthesis between the Lager and Levi's return to ordinary life: the nine-month odyssey of adventure and freedom. In historical terms, it refers to the period between World War II and the Cold War, between the threat of genocide and the threat of atomic apocalypse. In metaphysical terms, it refers to those oases of goodness and order, those moments of reprieve that sometimes condense out of the dark matter of the universe. It reflects the fundamental instability of a life that includes both unjustified suffering and salvation through laughter.

It is often hard in Levi's work to separate the desolation wrought by the Nazis from the desolation of a disenchanted, post-religious stage in western culture from the desolation of a depressive poet from the desolation of modern, industrial economies from the desolation of a universe that is naturally chaotic. What does it mean to say, as Levi does, in closing *Moments of Reprieve*, that "all of us are in the ghetto, that the ghetto is fenced in, that beyond the fence stand the lords of death, and not far away the train is waiting?"[52] Is life, in its basic parameters, really analogous to the life of the Jews in the Warsaw ghetto under the Nazis?

In the poem "The Black Stars," Levi writes: "Let no one sing again of love or war. / The order from which the cosmos took its name has been dissolved." For Levi, there has been a massive destruction, a negative creation that requires a new testament by a new "anti-epic" poet. Virgil wrote the creation story for Rome; he sang of arms and the man, of how the survivor from Troy founded a new order. But Levi never feels like a new Aeneas, carrying a brave new world with him as he travels back to Italy from the Lager. Rather he feels "a larger anguish, which was mixed up with our own misery, with the heavy, threatening sensation of an irreparable and definitive evil which was present everywhere, nestling like gangrene in the guts of Europe and the world, the seed of future harm."[53]

In dark moments, as in the 1983 essay "Brute Force," Levi sees the universe itself as maintained by a "perverse, not quite invincible force that prefers disorder to order, mixture to purity, confusion to parallelism, rust to iron, the heap to the wall and stupidity to reason."[54] We can erect only temporary stays against degradation: the world seems to be heading toward ruin, and we can only hope that the dissolution will be slow.[55] The decline afflicts individuals as it afflicts nature. Over the long run, as life destroys your defenses, you become another person: cowardly, nonresponsive, mean, corrupt, and a hypochondriac.[56]

More often, though, Levi sees a perpetual oscillation between heaven and hell, order and disorder, reason and unreason, comedy and tragedy. As Thomas Mann says, in one of Levi's favorite quotes, "Man is a confused creature."[57] Although Levi sometimes seems to be the consummate realist, the detached scientist, any account of his realism must be broad enough to include the fact that he often portrays competing realities cohabiting in such a way that one cannot wish one of them away as "only a dream." Neither reality can win a final battle. Sometimes one is dominant, at times the other; sometimes they coexist in an uneasy truce.

SEVEN

LIFE INSIDE THE LAW

L EVI SOMETIMES REFERRED to his time as a prisoner and a refugee as his "two years outside the law."[1] As different as they were, his experiences in Auschwitz and as a refugee were both highly anomalous, "experimental" situations. Their extreme nature made them highly revelatory about good and evil, but it left open the question of what humans are like in ordinary life: working, raising families, living "inside" the law.

For Levi, the process of rejoining normal life and finding himself as a worker, a family man, and a writer took place quickly and intensely in the two years after his return to Turin in October 1945. At first, he was in a feverish state, dealing with his memories of Auschwitz by writing poems, telling his story to everyone (even strangers on the tram) and then starting to write *If This Is a Man*. In January 1946, he found a job as a chemist at the DUCO paint factory in Avigliana, where he lived in a company dormitory and worked on his manuscript during breaks and at night (Levi said he wrote "The Canto of Ulysses" almost entirely during a half-hour lunch break).[2]

Meanwhile, although still haunted by memories of Vanda Maestro, Levi was looking for love. According to his old friend Gabriella Garda, within a few weeks of returning home, Levi told her that he had always loved her and asked her to leave her husband.[3] Gabriella turned him down but remained a good friend. Levi ends his story about her in *The Periodic Table* by noting that he and Gabriella share the curious impression that only a twist of fate had separated them: "a throw of the dice deflected us onto two divergent paths, which were not ours."[4] It is an odd sentiment, in part because, while Gabriella loved Levi, she was never attracted to him, but also because it reveals Levi's enduring detachment from his life, proceeding down a path he did not always feel to be his own.

Levi recovered from this disappointment and from the trauma of the war very quickly. He was finding success at work, his writing was going well, and then, on February 11, 1946, he went to a party where young people were celebrating the end of the war and dancing. Levi had never learned how to dance, and he asked a cousin to teach him. She did not know how either, but next to her stood Lucia Morpurgo, a schoolteacher, one year younger than Levi. Lucia offered to teach Levi to dance, and the two of them fell in love.[5]

In "Chromium," the climactic episode of *The Periodic Table*, Levi describes how everything came together when he met

Lucia—how, at long last, he became a true man, a fully human adult.

> Now it happened that the next day destiny reserved for me a different and unique gift: the encounter with a woman, young and made of flesh and blood, warm against my side through our overcoats, gay in the humid mist of the avenues, patient, wise and sure as we were walking down streets still bordered with ruins. In a few hours we knew that we belonged to each other, not for one meeting but for life, as in fact has been the case. In a few hours I felt reborn and replete with new powers, washed clean and cured of a long sickness, finally ready to enter life with joy and vigor; equally cured was suddenly the world around me, and exorcised the name and face of the woman who had gone down into the lower depths with me and had not returned.[6]

This lovely paragraph is saturated with gratitude toward Lucia for giving him a new life. In this baptism (he was "washed clean," "cured," and "reborn"), no one was trying to remake Levi or make him swallow an alien system; he was being freed to remake himself.

In a 1986 interview with Ferdinando Camon, Levi reflected on the effects of anti-Semitism, Auschwitz, and Lucia on his sense of manhood:

> No, as I said, Auschwitz was not simply negative for me, it taught me a lot. Among other things, before Auschwitz I was a man with no woman, afterwards I met the one who was to become my wife. I very much needed someone to listen to me, and she listened more than the others. That's why, in sickness and in health, I'm bound to her for life. Before that I was full of complexes, I don't know why. Maybe because I was a Jew. As

a Jew, I'd been made fun of by my schoolmates: not beaten up,
or insulted, but made fun of, yes.[7]

Ironically, while schoolboy anti-Semitism had emasculated
him, Auschwitz made him feel like a man, finally ready for
a woman, particularly one who would listen to him carefully
when he told his story. Not only did Lucia love him body and
soul, she also served as his key reader and editor as he wrote
If This Is a Man. Falling in love, Levi says, changed his writing
from the work of a convalescent begging for compassion to
the work of chemist, measuring and judging, trying to answer
questions, exalting in the work of finding the right word, con-
cise and strong. "Paradoxically," Levi writes, "my baggage of
atrocious memories became a wealth, a seed; it seemed to me
that, by writing, I was growing like a plant."[8] At last, Levi—the
mountaineer, inorganic chemist, man of rocks—had found a
fulfillment he could praise as organic.

Sadly, however, ordinary life was not to prove a paradise
to follow Levi's time in the inferno and purgatory. Rather, it
would be a blend, a coexistence, an uneasy truce between
the three states. Even the beautiful passage from *The Periodic
Table* cited above contains hints that there are limits to being
"washed clean." For example, it is odd that Levi says he "exorcised the name and face of the woman who had gone down
into the lower depths with me and not returned," referring to
Vanda Maestro. If Vanda's name and face truly had been exorcised, he would not be mentioning her now, letting her shade
darken the sunny mood. Moreover, Levi, the great memoirist,
the man whose atrocious memories had become a "wealth,"
would not want to banish Vanda like an evil spirit, even if he
could.

Apparently, the very night Levi met Lucia, he wrote her a love poem, "11 February 1946" which oddly parallels a poem he had written for Vanda several weeks earlier, "25 February 1944" (the date of Levi and Vanda's deportation to Auschwitz). In the poem to Vanda, Levi recalls how in their last days together, they longed to walk together once again beneath the sun.[9] In the poem for Lucia, Levi writes that, face to face with death at Auschwitz, he somehow felt her presence, even though he had not yet met her. She was there before him, beside him: they were together, a "man and woman under the sun," and he came back because she was there.[10] It is strange that, in Levi's imagination, Lucia—who spent the war in Italy—is with him at Auschwitz, where Vanda died. The overlapping poems suggest that, much as Levi would like to import Lucia's presence into the past, he is condemned to carry Vanda's absence into the future.

Levi wrote one other poem to Lucia during their engagement, "Avigliana"—named for the town where he worked at the DUCO plant, temporarily separated from her. The poem is beautiful, but slightly odd. Levi links Lucia to the fireflies, the "gentle dear little creatures," the "*lucciole*," whose name resembles hers, but he also distinguishes her from them. His way of appreciating them is to leave them alone. He ends the poem ambiguously, saying that if someday he and Lucia want to part, or if someday they want to marry, he hopes it will be like this evening in June, with the fireflies all around and Lucia not there.[11] It is an unusual love poem that contemplates both parting and getting married with equal poise.

In Levi's work as a chemist, as in his writing and his love life, the two years after his return were a highly-charged blend of failure, success, and growth. In 1946, as he was falling in love with Lucia and writing *If This Is a Man*, he had a major triumph at DUCO: he discovered a new antirust agent. But commuting to Avigliana and the daily grind and corporate politics of work at the paint factory frustrated Levi, and so, in June 1947, he quit DUCO to join his old university and mountaineering friend Alberto Salmoni as an independent chemist for hire.

His time with Alberto was rich in adventures and yielded three memoir-stories for *The Periodic Table* ("Arsenic," "Nitrogen," and "Tin"), in which Alberto becomes "Emilio." Levi liked to quote Pavese's stark dictum that the only two experiences of adult life are success and failure.[12] But while each Emilio story describes a failure, each also seems merry and triumphant. If Levi fails to extract usable alloxan from chicken shit ("the shit remained shit"), he succeeds in extracting a great story from the attempt.[13] As it turns out, these stories are not really from his adult life. They are from the last gasps of his prolonged adolescence, a last moment of reprieve: a marvelous time of integration when, as Levi once told an interviewer, his three lives of work, family, and writing interacted happily, and he felt full of energy and strength.[14]

Those exciting, improvisatory years could not last forever. In September 1947, Levi married Lucia, and she soon became pregnant, leading him to consider a more stable income for his family. In October 1947, Levi published *If This Is a Man* with Antonicelli, a small, anti-Fascist publisher in Turin (six other publishers had rejected it). But the response from the critics and the public was tepid, and there was no sign that his career as a writer, if he pursued it, would be remunerative. Work with Alberto was exciting, but not highly paid or reliable. And so

Levi put an end to their venture, and in April 1948 he began work at the SIVA paint and varnish factory, where he would stay until his retirement in 1977.

On some levels, Levi's career at SIVA was quite successful. He enjoyed the trust and friendship of the company's owner, Federico Accati, and, in 1953, Accati promoted him to technical director. The new job meant better pay and better hours, but it also meant spending less time in the laboratory, where Levi was happiest and most skilled, and more time doing administrative chores and handling personnel issues, where Levi was least fulfilled and least competent. By the time he retired, Levi was heartily sick of his job, describing it to a friend as "almost thirty years of forced labor."[15] At his retirement party, he said only this for a speech: "I believe I have always tried not to get on anyone's nerves."[16]

Generally, Levi had the trust and camaraderie of a staff that liked and respected him.[17] But by the time he retired, his distaste for disciplining workers, even when worker safety was at stake, had led his coworkers to conclude that he was no longer fit to run the plant.[18] Worse, in 1978, Levi, along with other managers, was charged with negligence toward the workers. The investigator said he was dangerously unprofessional and that, ironically, his experience at Auschwitz must have made him undervalue the gravity of the human situation at the factory.[19] Levi's eventual amnesty from the charges arose more from lenience and luck than from the merits of his case.

Before the Racial Laws and the war stymied him, Levi had dreamed of being an astrophysicist, not the technical director at a paint factory. He had dreamed of using science to find the essence of reality, not making products to apply to the surfaces of things. In their interview, when Philip Roth called him a scientist, Levi humbly corrected him: "By the way, I am not a scientist, nor have I ever been one. I did want to become one, but war and the camp prevented me. I had to limit myself to being a technician."[20] Levi went on to tell Roth that industrial chemistry was brutally incompatible with writing and involved many soul-destroying tasks.[21]

Levi once said that if he had not worked all those years at SIVA, he could not have written *The Periodic Table*. But all the tales of Levi's chemical exploits in *The Periodic Table* come from his schooling and from his first jobs: the mine, the Crescenzago factory, the DUCO plant, and especially from his year with Alberto Salmoni. Only three stories take place during his 30 years at the SIVA factory, and even those three barely touch on his work there. "Vanadium" is really a story about Auschwitz, framed in a fictional work context. "Uranium" is the tale of a rogue chemist from another company, Bonino, who tells Levi a ridiculous story, which, for all its stupidity, makes him envious: While Levi remains tangled in the net of duty— toward society, his company, and the truth—Bonino revels in the freedom of inventing his own past, making himself a hero and flying like Superman across space and time.[22] Rather than praising work, "Uranium" explores the ambiguous delights of irresponsible play and invention.

The story in "Silver" comes not from Levi's life at SIVA, but from an old university classmate whose chemical product gets spoiled by tiny pieces of lint from the workers' clothes; it is a story, writes Levi, "in which stolid matter manifests a cunning intent upon evil and obstruction."[23] He goes on to say that these episodes in the life of a chemist give one a sense of impotence, of an interminable war against an obtuse enemy.[24] This is the world of Mordo Nahum, the Greek, for whom work is war, not the joyous world of Cesare, for whom work is a game.

Levi believes that work is an essential part of one's bildungs-roman, with what he calls educational and formative value.[25] As he tells an interviewer, "[i]n work I found a Conradian view of life, the significance and the positive labour of struggling to reach an end. I saw the acceptance of responsibility, not its rejection, as the route to becoming adult."[26] One might ask in all sincerity, however, whether a "Conradian view of life" is a blessing, and whether Levi's rejection of despair sounds some-what desperate. He tells the interviewer:

> In myself, I am not despairing. For eight hours a day, I'm a technician, a man at war with the obtuse and malign inertia of matter; and you cannot fight a war in despair, since at least you have an end in sight.... However, I would not be able to give a full, explicit justification of this faith of mine in the future of mankind. It is a faith I would call biological...that has led mankind, despite innumerable errors, to the conquest of the planet. It may well not be rational, but then neither is despair. It solves no problem, in fact it makes some new ones and by its very nature it causes suffering.[27]

To think that matter is characterized by an "obtuse and malign inertia," is, perhaps, already to have despaired. It is hard to see how an attempt to conquer the planet could end in anything but defeat, how the hunt for the white whale—to use another of Levi's favorite metaphors for work—could end in anything but shipwreck.

Yet, Levi never gives up on work and never stops singing—however ambiguously—its praises. He tells an interviewer that humans are biologically wired to work toward goals, and that idleness or useless work (as in the Lager) leads to suffering and atrophy.[28] Work means being useful, and there are few things worse than being, or feeling, useless. In Levi's fable about suicide, "Westward," the character Anna describes depression as uselessness: "That hole. That void. That feeling... useless, with all around me useless, drowned in a sea of uselessness."[29]

Work counteracts the void; it is both natural and good. Nothing annoys Levi more than the facile assumption, whether derived from the Bible or misreadings of Marx, that work is by its nature punishment or alienation; and he especially resents comparisons of modern factories or other forms of labor to Auschwitz. Levi had experienced truly useless labor in the Lager: the Buna factory, where he worked, never produced a single kilo of rubber, despite all the efforts of the Nazis and their slaves. Most of the work in the Lager was not even designed to produce anything, but only to degrade, wear down, make docile, and eventually kill the inmates. As Levi rightly points out, working in an Italian factory in the 1970s was simply not comparable.

But the true opposite of slave labor is the kind of work Levi celebrates in *The Monkey's Wrench*, his first novel, composed in the period just before and after his retirement from SIVA in 1977. *The Monkey's Wrench* consists of a loosely linked set of work adventures told by a charming, globetrotting rigger, Faussone, to the narrator, an industrial chemist closely resembling Levi. Faussone, whose first name is "Libertino," exemplifies the kind of work that Levi believes in: autonomous problem solving, untethered by family or by bureaucracy. The Italian title, *La chiave a stella*, refers to a type of wrench, but literally it means "the star-shaped key": a poetic title indicating Levi's exalted conception of work as a key to the universe.

Levi said in an interview that he wrote *The Monkey's Wrench* partly with the aim of vindicating the nobility of work.

> I wanted to describe another human condition: not someone stuck in a repetitive job, as so many are in today's world, but someone who follows an ancient, timeless destiny, who measures himself against the world through his own work, who takes the risk of getting it wrong, who will try and try again an infinity of times until at last he gets it right, finds the answer, hits the target. Mine is precisely an idea of work as destiny, work as the human condition.[30]

In the novel itself, he writes, "If we except those miraculous and isolated moments fate can bestow on a man, loving your work (unfortunately, the privilege of a few) represents the best, most concrete approximation of happiness on earth."[31] Loving one's work is apparently the best thing in life, but notice the qualifications: only a few enjoy this privilege, and even for them it is only an "approximation" of happiness. Levi experienced this approximate happiness at various points in his life, particularly before and immediately after the war, when his work felt like conquest, adventure, and education. But for the bulk of his career, work occupied a grayer place in his cosmos, neither enslavement nor excitement: an oscillation between soul-enhancing and soul-destroying tasks.

Levi believed in doing his duty, but he was not necessarily inspired by it. Like his work, his home life involved some strenuous feelings of duty. He and his wife moved in with his mother a few months after their marriage in 1947, making a commitment to care for her that ended only with Levi's death 40 years later. Family obligations became even more onerous when Lucia's aged, visually impaired mother moved in down the hall.

In an essay entitled "My House," Levi makes a curious statement: "I have always lived (with involuntary interruptions) in the house where I was born, so my mode of living has not been the result of a choice."[32] It is odd to include the times he lived in Milan, at the mine, in the DUCO dormitories, and in the apartment he shared with Lucia right after their marriage as "involuntary," just as it is odd to portray his decision to move home as something other than a choice. Levi seems to regard his homebound life as something of a fatality, the opposite of freedom. He goes on to explain that his "static destiny" has given him a never-satisfied love for travel and has inspired the frequent motif of the journey in his books.[33]

Primo and Lucia Levi had two children, Lisa and Renzo, born in 1948 and 1957. Because Levi rarely, if ever, wrote about his children or about being a father, we know relatively little about that side of his life. The children took after him in at least some respects: both became scientists. Levi was a tender and gentle father who never got angry; his children provided him with much joy, especially when young, and he was particularly close to his daughter.[34] On the other hand, he may not have been the most attentive of parents, given that he was working full time at the factory while also writing prolifically. Also, Levi's

Auschwitz experience was something of a barrier between him and his children: he wanted them to know about it, and they wanted to know as little as possible about it; they wanted a normal father.[35]

Levi also did not write about himself as a husband, but apparently he was not a model spouse. He had two long-term affairs. The first, which took place from 1963 to 1968, was with a woman he later referred to as Lilith, after the legendary Jewish she-demon and temptress.[36] The second relationship, with a woman he called Gisella, lasted in some form from 1974 until his death in 1987.[37] In addition to suffering these affairs, Lucia also had to live in the home of a demanding mother-in-law and put up with Levi's deep immersion in his writing. In his poem for Lucia's sixtieth birthday, "12 July 1980," Levi rather cruelly refers to her as "weary," "impatient," "ground down," "mortified," and "flayed." But he is also apologetic and grateful, concluding that his lines are "my rough way of saying how dear you are, / And that I wouldn't be in this world without you."[38]

Levi did not write at all about the most central figure in his life, his mother, but he did sometimes complain—in conversations, letters, and even interviews—about the burden of caring for her. Things got particularly bad after his retirement in 1977, when both his mother's and mother-in-law's health became increasingly fragile, and he began turning down speaking engagements and travel opportunities because of them. His mother became increasingly depressed, something Levi himself found deeply depressing.[39] Even after he hired day and night nurses, he spent long hours at her bedside, and when he left she called out to him constantly.[40] According to one colleague, whenever Levi sat down to write, his mother would summon him by banging on the adjoining wall with her walking stick.[41]

An old friend said of his home life, "Primo was always a prisoner"; and a cousin said, more brutally, "Primo built himself a Lager."[42] The comparison may be offensive, but Levi himself could be quite harsh on the topic. In a passage from his interview with Germaine Greer that does not appear in *The Voice of Memory*, Greer talks about the skeletal, degraded people she had just seen in famine-struck Ethiopia, prompting Levi to say that he has "Ethiopians" in his own house—his mother and mother-in-law—and to compare the two women to the drowned victims of Auschwitz.[43]

Levi often rejects, and is even repulsed by, ideas of the factory as a Lager, the home as a Lager, or life as a Lager. But the poetry and depth of all his work depends on some kind of integration, however ambiguous and unstable, between his different worlds. Even Levi's most explicit messages depend on our realizing that, despite its uniqueness, Auschwitz is always a possibility slumbering in our current reality. As he writes in *The Drowned and the Saved*, the most urgent question is, how much of the Lager is back or coming back?[44] That is why understanding the gray zone is vital to comprehending "what takes place in a big industrial factory," and why "if from inside the Lager, a message could have seeped out to free men, it would have been this: take care not to suffer in your own homes what is inflicted on us here."[45]

Yet we must be careful in interpreting a home life about which we know so little, and careful not to generalize from comments Levi made when depressed. Levi lived the life he chose, and it enabled a long, prolific career as a writer. The two women with whom he had affairs were important readers of his draft work, but, then again, so was Lucia. His mother may have been somewhat cool and controlling, and she may have become a burden to him, but she must have done many things right in raising such a splendid human being as Levi. Levi may have regarded his home life as fated, rather than chosen, but he certainly viewed it as "his." As he says of his house, "I live in my house as I live inside my skin: I know more beautiful, more ample, more sturdy, and more picturesque skins; but it would seem to me unnatural to exchange them for mine."[46]

What is most characteristic in Levi's literary attitude toward his home life is not negativity but silence. When asked why he did not write about his mother, Levi told an interviewer that "you don't write about the living."[47] But Levi wrote about living friends like Alberto Salmoni and Lello Perugia all the time, just not about his family—or for that matter, any family. He wrote most often and most convincingly about friends, rivals, and enemies. He was captivated by voyages, no matter how often they ended in shipwreck—not by ordinary life at the SIVA factory or at home. As he told Philip Roth, "Family, home, factory are good things in themselves, but they deprived me of something that I still miss: adventure."[48]

The great battle of Levi's adult life was not one that he characterized as an adventure: it was his struggle with depression. It seems that his depression had biological roots and recurred regularly, although the timing and extent of it could be affected by situational factors such as illness, family unhappiness, work problems, and fears of not being able to write anymore. Levi himself cautions us against any confidence in assigning reasons for sadness, writing in *The Drowned and the Saved*:

> Anguish is known to everyone, even children, and everyone knows that it is often blank, undifferentiated. Rarely does it carry a clearly written label that also contains its motivation; any label it does have is often mendacious.[49]

It would be rash to speculate on how much, if any, of his depression was caused by Auschwitz. As he writes in one letter, "Auschwitz, perhaps? No, I do not think so, the camp belongs to a far too remote past, and moreover it has been exorcised by my books."[50] In his writing, the two experiences are linked not so much causally as metaphorically: he uses the same images of shipwreck to describe his depression that he uses to describe the fate of the drowned victims of the Nazis.

As we have seen, Levi suffered from various forms of despair in his youth and talked about suicide while still at university. In the 1940s, Levi was already writing great poetry about the sadness of daily life, as in "Crescenzago," from 1943, and "Monday," from 1946. "Monday" presents three images of sorrow: a train that leaves when it is supposed to, with only one voice and only one route; a cart horse stuck between two shafts, unable to look sideways; and a man who lives alone and believes that his time has run its course. The poem ends with a gentle version of Levi's dehumanizing idiom, saying that such a man is a sad "thing."

Levi suffered from major depressive episodes beginning in the 1950s, eventually leading him to consult a psychiatrist and to take antidepressants. He often fell into severe depressions after finishing books. In 1963, when he completed *The Truce*, he suddenly found himself sleeping badly, lacking a zest for life, and fearful that he had permanently depleted his fund of stories.[51] Similarly, after finishing *Vizio di forma* ("Structural defect"), a short story collection, in 1971, he felt a "cold inward deadness" and thought of suicide. "This is not the first time I have experienced such 'shipwrecks,'" he wrote to a friend, "but every time it seems to be final and definitive."[52]

For Levi, depression undid the work of self-mastery, of his ability to make himself a man. Because of a slight change in your hormonal balance, Levi wrote in a letter, "you are turned into *somebody else*."[53] In a later bout with depression he wrote to another friend, "I hope that you never experience such an alteration of the soul."[54] Depression undermined his power of reason: on a rational level, he knew that it would end, but his emotions overwhelmed him with the feeling that he would never find an exit.[55]

Like Auschwitz, depression opened the door to a terrible alternate reality, a dark void. Ironically, at Auschwitz, with chaos all around him, Levi's soul felt alive. He told Philip Roth:

> I remember having lived my Auschwitz year in a condition of exceptional spiritedness....I never stopped recording the world and people around me, so much that I still have an unbelievably detailed image of them. I had an intense wish to understand, I was constantly pervaded by a curiosity that somebody afterwards did, in fact, deem nothing less than cynical, the curiosity of the naturalist who finds himself transplanted into an environment that is monstrous but new, monstrously new.[56]

Depression, by contrast, deadened his will to live and his insatiable curiosity.

When Levi was not depressed, he felt completely different; he felt a strong love of life. Of all writers, he felt closest to the lusty, exuberant Rabelais, almost like a son: he told an interviewer that, if he could, he would choose Rabelais as a father.[57] Ferdinando Camon, who interviewed him extensively not long before he died, told him that he was not depressed or even anxious: he was someone who loved life. Interviewing him in his last year, Philip Roth described him as animated, nimble, and youthfully Pan-like.[58] However real Levi's depression was, it was not more real than his merriment and vitality.

Eight

Uncertain Hours

WHILE WORKING FULL time and caring for his family, Levi was also forging his third life, as a writer. Discouraged by the indifference that greeted the first edition of *If This Is a Man*, he wrote relatively little in the 1950s: a small number of stories and poems, and some draft sections for what became *The Truce*. In 1958, however, the prestigious publisher Einaudi agreed to publish a new edition of *If This Is a Man*, which proved the turning point in Levi's literary career. The new edition was a success, critically and popularly, and starting in the early 1960s Levi wrote prolifically until his death, experimenting in almost every genre and gradually winning an international reputation. Writing became the center of his life, and, not surprisingly, his thinking about writing became increasingly complex and rich.

Levi believed in stories as a path to truth, and, in particular, to truths about human nature. And while he differentiated scientific from literary truth, Levi retained a scientist's respect for reaching truth through close observation and accurate recording. Fittingly, then, Levi's greatest stories are his "true" stories. As he writes in the preface to *If This Is a Man*, "none of the facts are invented."[1] Even years after the events, he claims to remember them with uncanny accuracy, writing in *Moments of Reprieve* that he has not forgotten a single thing, that not a detail has been lost, and that he remembers like a tape recorder whole sentences in languages he does not even speak.[2]

The matter is not so simple, however, because Levi wrote all his stories as literature and often mixed fact with fiction. Many of the models for his characters complained, often bitterly, about the things he made up. Lello Perugia was angry at his transformation into Cesare in *The Truce*.[3] Sandro Delmastro's family was outraged by his depiction in *The Periodic Table*. Delmastro was from Turin, not the country; he was middle class, not poor; he did not spend his summers working as a shepherd.[4] Gabriella Garda, recast as "Giulia," did not threaten Levi that she would yell "Get your hands off me, you pig!" unless he gave her a ride; but when she asked Levi to remove the episode, he refused, telling her that it expressed her personality better than anything that really did happen.[5]

Levi feels free to use fiction because he is aiming not only for historical accuracy but also for deeper, more literary truths. As he writes in *Moments of Reprieve*, the people he portrays must "survive and enjoy the ambiguous perennial existence of literary characters."[6] To give them immortality, he needs to exaggerate, to round things out and heighten their colors;

without this alteration, he explains, one is not writing stories, but merely accounts.[7]

The older Levi's memories grew, the more literary they became. For example, he added one of the most literary chapters in *If This Is a Man*, "The Initiation," with its very dramatic presentation of Steinlauf, to the 1958 edition of the book. He added other characters, too—sympathetic ones, such as Schlome, the Polish Jewish boy who welcomes him to the Lager, and Chajim, the early bed companion whom he trusts blindly.[8] He also added the beautiful passages paying tribute to his friend Alberto. In general, the book became less bleak and more human, sympathetic, and literary.[9] It moved toward the *Moments of Reprieve* stories, which read more like short stories than memoirs and which in Italy were published alongside purely fictional tales in the collection *Lilít e altri racconti* ("Lilith and other stories").

This alteration of memory was somewhat involuntary. As Levi writes in *Moments of Reprieve*, the distance in time accentuated the tendency toward exaggeration.[10] He describes this tendency in more negative terms in *The Drowned and the Saved*:

Nevertheless, even under normal conditions a slow degradation is at work, an obfuscation of outlines, a so to speak physiological oblivion, which few memories resist. Doubtless one may discern here one of the great powers of nature, the same that degrades order into disorder, youth into old age, and extinguishes life in death. Certainly practice (in this case, frequent re-evocation) keeps memories fresh and alive in the same manner in which a muscle often used remains efficient, but it is also true that a memory evoked too often, and expressed in the form of a story, tends to become fixed in a stereotype, in a form tested by experience, crystallized, perfected, adorned, installing itself in the place of the raw memory and growing at its expense.[11]

Transmuting the dross of events into the gold of stories makes them enduring and beautiful, "crystallized, perfected, adorned," but also artificial. At its worst, this is how former Nazis justify their pasts: they fictionalize memories into stories and then repeat their stories until even they cannot remember the truth. At its best, this alchemy turns mere accounts into literature.

One of Levi's goals as a writer is to do justice to the people he encountered in his life. Writing about evil characters like Dr. Pannwitz, Alex the Kapo, and Adolf Eichmann, Levi balances the accounts. He labors just as hard to pay tribute to virtuous men, like Sandro Delmastro. In *The Periodic Table,* he says that it is impossible to write about Sandro: "He was not the sort of person you can tell stories about, nor to whom one erects monuments—he who laughed at all monuments: he lived completely in his deeds, and when they were over nothing of him remains—nothing but words, precisely."[12] And yet he writes about Sandro anyway, because, if nothing remains of him but words, it is vital to make the words as fitting as possible.

Not surprisingly, then, Levi's most memorable characters appear in his memoirs, not his pure fictions. In the two novels, *The Monkey's Wrench* and *If Not Now, When?,* he attempts character studies but fails to create figures nearly as interesting as Lorenzo, Cesare, Alberto, Sandro, Rappoport, or Rumkowski. In his short stories, Levi emphasizes symbolical, quasi-mythical situations over character development. Many of his "science fables" are variations on legends of man's disastrous, Faustian pride. Often, they concern the hubris of trying to make or remake a man; perhaps it is appropriate, then, that in none of them does Levi fashion men as vital as those in his memoirs.

Storytelling is a way to learn the truth, but it is also therapeutic. The epigraph to *The Periodic Table* is a Yiddish proverb, "Troubles overcome are good to tell." Even *If This Is a Man,* he writes in its preface, was written as an interior liberation, to satisfy a violent impulse.[13] The intention to leave an eyewitness account was secondary.[14] Hence, Levi tells us, its fragmentary character: the fact that the chapters were written not in logical succession, but in order of urgency.[15] Hence, one might add, some of its modernity: the way it eschews a seamless narrative in favor of a more subjective, disjunctive form.

Writing as therapy may seem quintessentially modern, and, in an interview with Ferdinando Camon, Levi compares it to lying down on Freud's couch.[16] And yet, as we have seen, Levi is not a classically Freudian writer. If he seeks therapy for individual neuroses, he also, more importantly, seeks therapy for the radical evil inflicted by the Nazis. And Levi seeks his cure through the pure act of storytelling—including, crucially, finding a good listener—not by having his story analyzed by an expert. The act of remembering and telling is itself healing: Levi writes in *The Periodic Table* that "calling up a moment of anguish in a tranquil mood, seated quietly at one's desk, is a source of profound satisfaction."[17]

Unfortunately, literature was not always healing; sometimes it was traumatic. In 1982 Levi accepted a commission from his publisher, Einaudi, to translate *The Trial* for a "Writers Translated by Writers" series. His engagement with Kafka turned into something of a Kafkaesque nightmare, as he describes in an interview:

> I felt assaulted by this book and I had to defend myself. Precisely because it is a marvelous book that runs you through like a spear, like an arrow...I do not love him, I admire him, I fear him, like a great machine that crashes in on you, like the prophet who tells you the day you will die.[18]

Levi tries to defend himself, proclaiming his difference from Kafka. According to Levi, Kafka writes about his own hallucinations and never helps the reader to understand what they mean. Levi, by contrast, tries to resolve problems, rather than give free reign to his subconscious.[19] This is somewhat convincing, at least as it applies to Levi's nonfiction. But notice what happens as Levi continues the interview:

> We had very different fates. Kafka grew up in very serious conflict with his father; he was the product of three intermingled cultures, Jewish, German, and the culture of Prague. He was unhappy in his emotional life, frustrated in his work, and in the end seriously ill. He died young. I, on the other hand, despite the episode of the Lager, which marked me deeply, have had a different life, a less unhappy life. My own personal happy ending, that fact of having survived the camps, made me stupidly optimistic. Today, I am less of an optimist. At that time I was more so. At that time I committed an illogical transfer of my own personal happy ending—which enriched me, by making me a writer—on to all human tragedies.[20]

Levi's attempt to distinguish himself from Kafka is curiously unpersuasive. After all, Levi, too, grew up in conflict with his father and was the product of intermingled cultures; he too was often unhappy in his emotional life, frustrated in his work, and "in the end seriously ill," in his case, with depression. Levi differentiates himself from Kafka mainly by saying that he is more optimistic, but goes on to say that his optimism was misplaced, and that he now agrees with Kafka's pessimism: his strange gift that goes beyond reason and his almost animal-like sensitivity, like snakes that know when earthquakes are coming.[21]

In other words, Levi casts himself as being somewhat like the child whom he says he would protect from reading the ending of The Trial.

> Now this ending is so cruel, so unexpectedly cruel, that if I had a young child I would spare him. I fear it would disturb him, make him suffer, although of course it is the truth. We will die, each of us will die, more or less like that.[22]

Similarly, in his essay "Translating Kafka," Levi both distances himself from and identifies with Kafka, for whom he proclaims an ambivalent love, close to fear and rejection. He writes that he admires Kafka for writing in a way that is totally unavailable to him. In his writing, Levi has always tried to pass from darkness into light, like a filtering pump sucking up dark, dirty water and expelling it purified, possibly sterile.[23] Kafka, by contrast, sucks you into his black hole.

> His suffering is genuine and continuous, it assails you and does not let you go: you feel like one of his characters, condemned by an abject and inscrutable, tentacular tribunal that invades the city and the world...or transformed into a clumsy and cumbersome insect, disliked by all, desperately alone, obtuse,

incapable of communicating or thinking, capable at this point only of suffering.[24]

Levi had suffered both of these Kafkaesque experiences: like K., he was sentenced to die by a senseless tribunal that invaded the world and, like Gregor Samsa, he was struck by an enigmatic power (depression) that made him feel like an insect, desperately alone, good only for suffering. In the preface to his translation of *The Trial,* Levi describes K. in way that closely resembles his portrayal of himself and the other inmates at Auschwitz: "His dignity as a man is compromised right from the start, and then willfully and determinedly demolished day by day."[25]

Levi had also experienced the primordial shame that Kafka attributes to K. at the end of *The Trial,* in the phrase "it was as if the shame of it must outlive him." In his essay "Translating Kafka," Levi writes that this famous sentence, which closes the book like a tombstone, is not enigmatic to him. K., he says, is ashamed of many contradictory things, because he himself is contradictory: his essence, like that of almost all of us, consists of being incoherent, not equal to himself. He continues:

> ...in this shame I sense another component that I know: Joseph K., at the end of his anguished journey, experiences shame because there exists this occult, corrupt tribunal that pervades everything surrounding him....It is in the end a human, not a divine tribunal: it is composed of men and made by men, and Joseph K. with the knife already planted in his heart is ashamed of being a man.[26]

All his life, Levi resisted Kafka's conclusion that to be a man is an inherently shameful, inhuman fate, but he suffered from dark moments in which he suspected that it was true. With the ambiguity of a great poet, he distilled his love of life and his anguish into unstable, but very rich, compounds.

Levi's attitude toward Kafka closely resembles his attitude toward his own poetry. Levi wrote poetry throughout his life, but he did not put his poems into book form until 1970, when he printed a private edition of 300 copies for friends, and then in 1975, when the Milanese publisher Scheiwiller released a collection of 27 poems called *The Beer-Hall of Bremen*. In 1984, Levi published a larger collection under the title *At an Uncertain Hour*. These two collections have been combined and translated into English as *Collected Poems*.

Levi's poetry drew few reviews and is still underrated. His usual publisher, Einaudi, rejected *At an Uncertain Hour* as "insufficiently distinguished."[27] But this critical neglect is easy to understand, given Levi's own surprisingly negative opinion of his poetry. As he told an interviewer:

> In my view, their value is minimal. My natural state is that of not writing poetry, but every now and then I get this curious infection, like an exanthematic illness that gives you a *rash*. I'd never write poetry methodically. I have on occasion written five or six in the span of two or three days.... It is happening now for I don't know what reason, perhaps because I have more free time, but it is quite out of my control. At some point you discover the kernel of a poem within you, the first line or one line, then the rest follows. Sometimes it works, other times I throw them away, but it's a phenomenon I don't understand, that I don't know about or know how to think about, whose

mechanics I reject. It's not part of my world. My world is one of thinking about something, developing it almost . . . like a rigger, yes, building it up bit by bit. The other method of producing by way of flashes of inspiration amazes me.[28]

"Exanthematic" is a particularly wonderful word; it means an eruptive disease, like the measles, but it comes from a Greek root, *exanthema*, which means to bloom or flower. Levi's poetry is often darker and more depressive but also more organic than his prose. Levi distrusts his poetry because it is wild; he would rather work like the hero of *The Monkey's Wrench*, a rigger, who thinks and builds with careful control, than like Kafka, following the threads of hallucinations and visions.

Even in his more positive depictions of poetry, Levi emphasizes its ungovernability and morbidity. In the surreal story "The Fugitive," Pasquale is a poet whose poems come to him like an epileptic fit. He writes his most beautiful poem, "Annunciation," only to have the piece of paper on which it is written, the "fugitive," magically hide and disintegrate, leaving only fragments that he can never reconstruct. The narrator discusses how all poetry is fugitive:

> To compose a poem that is worth reading and remembering is a gift of destiny: it happens to only a few people, without regard for rules or intentions, and to them it happens only a few times in their lives. Perhaps this is a good thing; if the phenomenon were more frequent, we would be drowning in poetic messages, our own and those of others, to the detriment of us all.[29]

Note the apparently casual use of the word "drowning," with its resonance of passivity, despair, and death.

As this story suggests, Levi was tormented by fear of writer's block, of losing his inspiration, a condition to which poets are particularly vulnerable. Despite his almost unstinting fertility, all his depressions seem to have included fears of not writing again, or not writing well. During a depression in 1982, Levi wrote a poem, "To the Muse," which he never published, perhaps because it was so frightening. In it, he complains to the Muse for visiting him so rarely and warns her that, if she does not hurry, she will find him enraged, insane, or dead.[30]

Levi also harbored a prejudice against poetry that may have dated to his school days, when Fascist ideology privileged poetry over science. In the chapter titled "Iron" in *The Periodic Table* he describes the periodic table as "poetry, loftier and more solemn than all the poetry we had swallowed down in *liceo*."[31] This resembles a similar complaint in the chapter "Potassium," about revealed truths as opposed to proven ones: "After having been force fed in *liceo* the truths revealed by Fascist doctrine, all revealed, unproven truths either bored me stiff or aroused my suspicion."[32] Poetry necessarily traffics in revelations, not proofs, and so it may have struck Levi as inherently specious.

Levi prized lucidity, and poetry lends itself to obscurity. In 1976, he published a controversial essay titled "On Obscure Writing." Bravely, Levi does not choose writers who write obscurely and badly; rather, he tackles three great writers: Ezra Pound, Paul Celan, and Georg Trakl. Not coincidentally, all three were poets, all three suffered from mental illness, and two took their own lives. Levi writes that a mentally ill writer should be respected and cured, but he must not be praised or held up as an example, because it is better to be sane than insane.[33] His logic falters here; most of us would rather be sane

than insane, but many great writers, including Levi, have suffered from severe mental illness without its disqualifying them
from praise.

Levi acknowledges that Pound may have been a great poet,
but he is convinced that Pound's obscurity has the same root
as his Fascism: his belief in supermen and his contempt for
the reader.[34] This rings false as a description of Pound, whose
contempt, however revolting, does not seem directed at readers; but it does help explain some of Levi's own feelings. Levi is
profoundly democratic: he believes that the author and reader
should meet as equals, making a contract, and that if the
reader does not understand, he feels unjustly humiliated, and
the writer is guilty of a "breach of contract."[35] But Levi's view
seems uncharacteristically narrow. An author and a reader
might make a contract for work that is difficult to understand
but enjoyable, meaningful, and perhaps an accurate reflection
of experiences that are themselves enigmatic.

Levi goes on to discuss Celan and Trakl:

> The effable is preferable to the ineffable, the human word to the
> animal whine. It is not by chance that the two least decipher-
> able poets writing in German, Trakl and Celan, both died as
> suicides.... Their common destiny makes one think about the
> obscurity of their poetry as a pre-suicide, a not-wanting-to-be,
> a flight from the world, of which the intentional death was the
> crown.[36]

Despite this somewhat brutal language, Levi has great respect
for Celan's poetry, which he calls tragic and noble.[37] Unlike
Pound, Celan is not willfully abstruse because of contempt for
his reader; rather, his obscurity reflects that of his fate and

of his generation.[38] Nonetheless, Levi finds Celan destructive rather than therapeutic:

> This darkness grows from page to page until the last inarticulate babble consternates like the rattle of a dying man, and that is just what it is. It attracts us as chasms attract us, but at the same time it also defrauds us of something that should have been said and was not, and so it frustrates and turns us away. I believe that Celan the poet should be meditated upon and pitied rather than imitated . . . it is not a communication, it is not a language, or at most it is a dark and truncated language precisely like that of a person who is about to die and is alone, as we all will be at the point of death. But since we the living are not alone, we must not write as if we were alone.[39]

As with Kafka, part of Levi's problem with Celan is not that he communicates obscurely, but that he communicates all too clearly feelings of obscurity: darkness, isolation, despair, and drowning.

Levi has a didactic side. He wants his writing to clarify and help the world, not simply to express a private anguish. He wants to transmute his passive suffering at the hands of the Nazis into an active involvement in history. He wants to contribute to the reasoned discourse that opposes violence, fascism, ignorance, prejudice, and other social ills. But poetry is not reasoned, lucid discourse: it is, according to Levi's essay "Rhyming on the Counterattack," violence done to everyday language.[40] In "On Obscure Writing," Levi states that writing becomes more valuable the less it lends itself to equivocal interpretations.[41] Poetry, by its very essence, is equivocal; it harbors ambiguities that cannot be resolved, depths that cannot be fathomed.

In other moods, Levi celebrates this aspect of writing. In *The Monkey's Wrench*, he writes that one of the author's great privileges is to remain imprecise, to say and not say, to invent freely, beyond any rule of caution.[42] In the essay "Writing a Novel" he says that a believable character must be "inconsistent, as we all are."[43] But this revolt against rational lucidity is exactly what makes Levi, in his more prosaic moods, so uncomfortable. Poetry, like obscure writing, sometimes strikes Levi as a siren call from the depths, attracting us the "way chasms attract us."[44] It issues too often from the mouths of bad teachers: Fascists like Pound and shipwrecked victims like Celan.

Levi's feelings about poetry relate to his feelings about Auschwitz. His first poetic outpouring came in the months after his return and includes seven great poems about the Lager. Levi's poems confront Auschwitz in a different, more intense way than his prose. For example, in "For Adolf Eichmann" he voices the desire for Eichmann to suffer eternally, a violent emotion he scrupulously avoids in his prose. "The Survivor" expresses a nightmarish guilt more visceral than the shame portrayed in his memoirs. "Shemà" contains a ferocity toward the reader that contrasts sharply with Levi's typical understated, respectful appeal. In "25 February 1944," he expresses his grief over Vanda's murder more openly than anywhere else.

If This Is a Man, The Truce, and *Moments of Reprieve* are all prefaced with poems about Auschwitz. Clearly, Levi believed that his poems contained some essential part of his thinking about his experiences there, but he still felt ambivalent about the way the poems came to him. Poetry, like memories of Auschwitz, came to Levi unbidden, at an "uncertain hour." The phrase "at an uncertain hour," which Levi uses repeatedly, comes from Coleridge's "Rime of the Ancient Mariner":

> Since then, at an uncertain hour
> That agony returns:
> And till my ghastly tale is told,
> This heart within me burns.

One of Levi's interviews includes this passage explaining what he means by an "uncertain hour":

> At an uncertain hour, that is, every now and again... It is not as though I live my life inside that world. Otherwise I would never have written *The Wrench*, I would never have had a family, I would never do many other things that give me pleasure. But it is true, at an uncertain hour, those memories return. I'm a recidivist.[45]

The word "recidivist" expresses some of the shame that these hours bring. The explanation reminds one of Levi's battle with depression, which also struck him at an uncertain hour. Poetry is like an illness, like an epileptic fit, like depression; it comes unbidden from the depths; it often drags one down into them. Writing poetry apparently did not make Levi happy. By contrast, he called the year he spent researching *If Not Now, When?*, his most prosaic work, "happy," "liberating," and "good fun."[46]

One might expect that Levi would have found putting together his personal anthology, *The Search for Roots,* as enjoyable as writing a novel, but, interestingly, he found it more like writing poetry. He writes in the introduction, "while writing in the first person is for me, at least in my intention, the work of day and conscious lucidity, I am aware that the choice of one's roots is more nocturnal work, visceral and for the most part unconscious."[47] In making this book he feels naked, as if he were opening himself up, "like Mohammed in the ninth pit and in the illustration by Doré, in which moreover the masochistic satisfaction of the damned is enormous."[48] But if the search for roots has some of poetry's subterranean, hellish quality, one might also say that poetry has some of the nourishing, vital quality of the search for roots.

In *The Periodic Table*, Levi offers a beautiful description of what writing meant to him upon his return from the war:

> The things I had seen and suffered were burning inside of me; I felt closer to the dead than the living, and felt guilty at being a man, because men had built Auschwitz, and Auschwitz had gulped down millions of human beings, and many of my friends, and a woman who was dear to my heart. It seemed to me that I would be purified if I told its story, and I felt like Coleridge's Ancient Mariner, who waylays on the street the wedding guests going to the feast, inflicting on them the story of his misfortune. I was writing concise and bloody poems... [B]y writing I found peace for a while and felt myself become a man again, a person like everyone else, neither a martyr nor debased nor a saint: one of those people who form a family and look to the future rather than the past.[49]

The problem is that writing is a very strange way to attempt to become "a person like everyone else." Telling his story does not completely purify the Ancient Mariner; if it did, the need to tell it would not keep coming back, in the agony of the uncertain hour. To write about one's suffering is to understand and conquer it, but it is also to relive and memorialize it: to define oneself by it and write it into one's soul.

Levi sometimes analogized his writing to his scientific work. In "The Writer Who Is Not a Writer," he compares writing to laboratory instruments and claims that his model is the weekly factory report: clear, to the point, comprehensible to everybody.[50] In *The Periodic Table,* he compares an author to a chemist who weighs, divides, measures, and judges on the basis of assured proofs.[51] Levi wanted to write about Auschwitz, the world's chaos, and depression from the outside in, bringing light and order to the void. But a writer is not a god. You can write a beautiful, orderly description of a black hole, but, when you are done, the black hole remains. Furthermore, it is not always true that evil is chaotic and writing orderly. If that were true, then Levi would not have borne such a love for Rabelais, whose style he calls joyful and good precisely because it is "incoherent, capricious, multicolored, full of surprises."[52]

For Levi, writing was both vital and fatal; it made him feel sometimes like Rabelais, and sometimes like Kafka. He found it therapeutic, even essential for life: He told Ferdinando Camon, "If you stop up my mouth, I die."[53] But he also experienced writing as a series of deaths. His poem "The Work," from 1983, ends with the line "[w]ith every work that's born you die a little": as if the writer had only a limited supply of vital matter in his soul, and, with each work, he gave some of it away, until finally his store was depleted, and he died.[54]

But if completing a tale can be fatal to the teller, so can failing to complete it. In *If This Is a Man* Levi narrates a dream he had in Auschwitz about the failure of storytelling. He dreamed that he was back home, and that he was telling the story of the Lager to his sister and some friends. He felt an intense, physical pleasure at recounting his story until he noticed that his listeners did not follow him. They were completely indifferent; even his sister got up and walked away without a word. The dream continues:

> A desolating grief is now born in me, like certain barely remembered pains of one's early infancy. It is pain in its pure state, not tempered by a sense of reality and by the intrusion of extraneous circumstances, a pain like that which makes children cry; and it is better for me to swim once again up to the surface...[55]

Levi links this dream to another common Lager dream, the dream of eating. As he writes in "The Writer Who is Not a Writer," food placed beyond one's grasp and the tale stopped before its end create the same anguish.[56]

To tell one's story is as basic a need as eating, and not being listened to is as basic a pain as hunger or the infant's feeling of abandonment. Not to have a story to tell, to lack more stories to tell, to be silenced by evil, or to be ignored by one's audience, are all lethal fates. Levi sometimes despaired that he had finished his work, and sometimes that it was impossible to finish his work: impossible, for example, to warn an indifferent humanity about the eminently (and imminently) repeatable devastation of the Lager, or impossible to write a testament that would offer hope.

Levi's real home was in literature, where success and failure commingle promiscuously and ambiguities cannot be resolved into pure solutions. Even his relationship to literature was a distillation of love and antagonism. At the end of his life, he told an interviewer: "When I was at school, I had a polemical relationship to literature. Later it became clear that it was love, resisted like all great loves."[57] A story is not a solution; it is a failure, one that must be told "with the humility and restraint of him who knows from the start that his theme is desperate, his means feeble, and the trade of clothing facts in words is bound by its very nature to fail."[58] But if failing is essential to staying human—a guarantee of humility and depth—then failure may be tinged with triumph.

In *The Periodic Table*, Levi offers a description of the chemical process of distillation, which also functions as a description of writing.

> Distilling is beautiful. First of all, because it is a slow, philosophic, and silent occupation, which keeps you busy but gives you time to think about other things...Then, because it involves a metamorphosis from liquid to vapor (invisible), and from this once again to liquid; but in this double journey, up and down, purity is attained, an ambiguous and fascinating condition, which starts with chemistry and goes very far. And finally, when you set about distilling, you acquire the consciousness of repeating a ritual consecrated by the centuries, almost a religious act, in which from the imperfect material you obtain the essence, the *usia*, the spirit, and in the first place alcohol, which gladdens the spirit and warms the heart.[59]

Distilling is how the mature Levi chooses to "obtain the essence," to reach the "spirit" that inheres in matter. Distilling involves a double metamorphosis, up and down, to reach an ambiguous purity. In his writing, Levi uses trial and error and restless experimentation to distill the most essential parts of his experience, oscillating from the particular to the general and back again, in search of a moral and aesthetic purity that maintains its ambiguity. As the ending reference to alcohol—spirits—shows, Levi's search for purity does not involve renouncing earthly things; he seeks, through chemistry and literature, both transcendence and immanence.

NINE

THE THAW

I N SOME WAYS, Levi's life and his universe remained static from the late 1940s—when he got married, moved back in with his mother, and joined the SIVA factory— until his death in 1987. His adventures were over, and all that remained was to write about them. Although he became one of Italy's best-known writers, his increasing fame did not alter his daily life very much: He stayed at the factory for 30 years, he rarely traveled, and he socialized mostly with old friends. Yet, as we read the stories, essays, and poems, we see that his cosmos continued to evolve—most strikingly, in his long and difficult embrace of the organic, the feminine, and the earthly.

Levi had always been suspicious of purity. In *The Periodic Table*, when he describes his crush on Rita, a gentile classmate, he portrays purity as "disgustingly moralistic" and identifies it with the Fascists. He is proud to be Jewish—the grain of impurity—just as he is proud to have held Rita's arm. He says that immaculate virtue, if it exists, is detestable.[1] Despite its title's suggestion of something elemental and systemic, *The Periodic Table* itself is a remarkable hybrid, a fertile mishmash blending autobiography, fiction, fantasy, science, and history into something new.

In the story "The Sixth Day," in which celestial bureaucrats discuss how to create a man, one rebukes the other:

> "...these attempts of yours to produce Superbeasts, all brain and balance, filled *ab ovum* with geometry, music, and wisdom, would make a cat laugh. They smacked of antiseptic and inorganic chemistry. For anyone with a certain experience of the things of this world, or for that matter of any other world, their incompatibility with the environment surrounding them would have been easily intuited, an environment that is of necessity both florid and putrid, pullulating, confused, changeable."[2]

Making a man—himself—is in some sense Levi's lifelong project, both as a person and as a writer, but he is constantly aware of the potential for hubris and naiveté. Much as he yearns to make himself a Platonic king filled with geometry, music, and wisdom, he knows that real men must live in the "putrid, pullulating, confused, and changeable" world of becoming and dying. Life is not geometric; as Levi writes in his essay "Asymmetry and Life": "asymmetry is intrinsic to life, and indeed it coincides with life."[3]

In *The Truce*, written in the early 1960s, Levi had done some justice to the organic world, with his celebrations of Cesare, the Russians, and other wild men, but he had remained suspicious of women and nature. Gradually, however, his writing grew closer to both. In the early 1980s, Levi's increased interest in the organic resulted in a slew of poems about flora and fauna, including ants, gulls, trees, spiders, moles, mice, oysters, snails, and elephants. One of his last poems, "The Thaw," offers a lovely culmination to this trend. Levi describes how, after the snow melts, an unidentified "we" will search for an old path behind a monastery's walls. There we will find certain rare herbs, good for curing melancholy. The tender ferns barely push up off the ground, but they are "ready for their loves," which are "more intricate than ours." Their germs, the tiny males and females, are ready to erupt at the first rain: to swim. "Long live the bride and groom!" Levi exclaims. We are tired of winter and the frost that has left its mark on us. We are ready for the thaw.[4]

Levi's universe, initially dominated by men and rocks, has changed dramatically. The poet is ready to celebrate the tiny, frail male and female "germs," to move beyond monastic purity and find a cure for his melancholy in love. In biographical terms, this embrace of the erotic may relate to Levi's second love affair: the one with Gisella. According to his confidantes, Gisella was generous and loving, and she and Levi shared happiness and a deep spiritual communion.[5] But Levi's thaw is also the fruit of a lifelong, arduous, never-completed attempt to find communion with the organic world.

Not just in his poems, but also in his short essays, Levi paid increasing attention to flora and fauna as he grew older. His 1985 collection, *Other People's Trades*, includes a number of pieces about animals. In the essay "Novel Dictated by Crickets," Levi writes:

> If I were able to, I would...fill my house with all sorts of animals. I would make an effort not only to observe them, but also to enter into communication with them. I would not do this for a scientific purpose...but out of affection, and because I am certain that from it I would derive an extraordinary spiritual enrichment and a more complete vision of the world. For lack of better, I read with ever-renewed enjoyment and amazement many books, old and new, that talk about animals, and I feel that I draw from them a vital nourishment, independent of their literary or scientific value. They may even be full of lies, like old Pliny: it doesn't matter, their value lies in the suggestions they offer.[6]

Levi uses many cosmic keywords in this apparently casual passage: "communication," "affection," "spiritual enrichment," "vital nourishment," and "more complete vision of the world." Characteristically, though, he does not fill his house with animals, but with books about animals. As we saw earlier, he prefers "the human word to the animal whine."[7] Only humans are truly loveable, because only they are capable of reason and discourse. Levi still finds animals both attractive and repulsive. He ends the essay with a gruesome description of how certain male spiders paralyze and rape their mates, while certain female spiders kill and devour the males.

Even in what seems like a very light essay, "Beetles," Levi's bleaker perspective resurfaces. He begins with an old joke: When biologist J. B. S. Haldane was asked by a churchman about the nature of God, he answered, "He is inordinately fond of beetles."[8] As usual, Levi's concerns are cosmic, even when joking. After surveying some facts about beetles, Levi writes:

> All these modes of behavior evoke a complex range of impressions: amazement, curiosity, admiration, horror, and laughter. But it seems to me that over them all predominates the sensation of extraneousness or alienation: these small flying fortresses, these portentous little machines, whose instincts were programmed one hundred million years ago, have nothing at all to do with us....[9]

From the seemingly neutral world of biology, we have entered the alienated cosmos of Kafka: the beetles are "the different ones, the aliens, the monsters. Kafka's atrocious hallucination is not chosen by chance."[10]

Luckily, the beetle coexists with the butterfly, the animal that gave the Greeks their name for the soul, the *psyche*. As Levi writes in "Butterflies," they were not made for the pleasure of man; they preexisted us by millions of years.[11] And yet they are not alien; in fact, our notion of beauty is patterned on them, as it is on the stars, the mountains, and the sea. The butterflies' beauty is not absolute, as we find when we examine them under a microscope. Then the "enormous eyes without pupils, the horn-like antennae, the monstrous, juglike mouth, look to us like a diabolical mask, a distorted parody of the human face."[12] But both sides of nature's Janus face are real, and the butterfly's mysterious beauty may even help reconcile us to nature's most petrifying visage: death. Levi ends the essay with a passage about Hermann Hesse's diary: On its last page, Hesse describes a rare butterfly that lands on his hand. Levi calls this "an ambivalent annunciation" with the "flavor of a serene presage of death."[13]

Levi felt a double bond, an impossible love, an unstable mixture of attraction and repulsion, for the world. Soon after he finished *The Periodic Table* in 1974, he began contemplating a sequel, *The Double Bond*, which would interweave memoir and fiction with explanations of organic chemistry, as *The Periodic Table* did with inorganic chemistry. Levi worked sporadically on the book, returning to it in earnest after publishing *The Drowned and the Saved* in 1986. He drafted five or six chapters that he showed to friends, family, an editor at Einaudi, and his lover, Gisella. It is an insoluble question whether Levi was unable to finish *The Double Bond* because it was impossible, or whether, if his life had not been cut short, he could have completed it. On the one hand, the title itself refers to an impossible task. On the other hand, while it took Levi years to write *The Periodic Table*, he managed it in the end.

"Unfinished Business," a poem from 1981, can be read as a meditation on the difficulty of writing *The Double Bond*. In it, the speaker submits his resignation from an unidentified job. He notes that he has left a great deal of uncompleted work, whether from laziness or practical problems, and asks to be forgiven. Above all, he had planned a marvelous book that would have "revealed innumerable secrets," "alleviated pain and fear," and "dissolved doubts," giving many people the gift of tears and laughter. It would have been a "fundamental work."[14] The reader may wonder whether anyone could really write such a book; it sounds like a new gospel, a kind of good news unavailable to a modern skeptic like Levi.

Levi intended *The Double Bond* to be a fundamental work, but on a very human scale. In the drafts, a chemist writes letters to a lady, *la Signora*, on wide ranging "organic" topics such as mayonnaise, internal organs, depression, sexuality, love, and death. Perhaps Levi's love affair played a role in inspiring the relationship of the chemist and the lady in the novel. In one draft, the book opens: "For fifteen years, Z. had been living in sin, and he knew it."[15] Interestingly, though, Z.'s sin is not philandering but polluting—he has been allowing toxic waste to spew from the factory he owns. Levi had firsthand experience: his SIVA factory had been dumping acetic acid into the sewage system for fifteen years. The dreamed-about purity of inorganic chemistry had, in its applications, created lethal impurities.

In his nonfiction, Levi tends to portray science as a noble venture to understand the cosmos, but in his fiction it is more often a Faustian, destructive attempt to reengineer nature. In the story "Angelic Butterfly," a German scientist working under the Nazi regime discovers that man has the potential to metamorphose to a higher stage, but his attempt to make angels results in hideous, doomed, vulturelike beings. In "Some Applications of the Mimer," the narrator describes Gilberto (who has just used a fantastical machine called the Mimer to duplicate his wife) as follows:

> That is Gilberto, a dangerous man, a small noxious Prometheus: he is ingenious and irresponsible, arrogant and foolish. He is a child of the century, as I have said before. Indeed, he is a symbol of our century. I've always thought that, if the occasion arose, he would have been able to build an atom bomb and drop it on Milan "to see the effect it would have."[16]

Levi refers to the atomic bomb in another story of a miraculous invention, "Versamina," which deals with a drug that can turn pain into pleasure. It is, says a character,

> "somewhat like the business of the Hiroshima bomb and the others that came later. It is not by chance, you see, not by chance: some believe they can free humanity from pain, others that they can give it energy gratis, and they do not know that nothing is gratis, ever: everything must be paid for."[17]

Strikingly, Levi ends *If Not Now, When?* with the characters attending the birth of a baby boy and then reading a newspaper headline about Hiroshima. The nuclear bomb is, like Nazism, a fundamental cosmic change. As Levi writes in the essay "Eclipse of the Prophets," it is something new in human history that a single act of will, a single gesture, could destroy the human species.[18] As a result of this new situation, certainty is impossible. We must build our own tomorrow, Levi says, gropingly, blindly, from the roots, resisting the temptation to recompose the shards of the old idols or build new ones.[19]

In this new search for roots, or rebuilding from the roots, we can learn from the trees, which are not as unlike us as we might think. As a girl in the story "Mutiny" says, trees are "people like us."[20] The poem "Wooden Heart" is about Levi's "next-door neighbor" on Corso Re Umberto, a robust horse chestnut that is Levi's age but doesn't look it. The tree harbors sparrows and blackbirds and is not ashamed of its sexuality: putting forth its buds and leaves, its fragile flowers. The tree has a hard life: deafened by noise, poisoned by the methane in the subsoil, watered with dog urine, and clogged with septic dust. Under its bark hang dead chrysalises that will never be butterflies. And yet, in its sluggish wooden heart, it still savors the spring's

return. The spring thaw is as inevitable as the winter that pre-
cedes it.[21]

A thaw can be permanent, or close to permanent, as when
an ice age, or a Cold War, ends. But more often, a thaw is sea-
sonal, part of the eternal but eternally changing weather. Levi
often experienced a tormented oscillation between heaven and
hell, but, strange as it seems, that oscillation is part of the natural order.[22] Hope and despair, life and death, *Lebenslust* and suicide are equally irrational, and hence equally rational; they are
part of nature and part of us. One will never conquer the other,
just as we will never conquer nature. Our words will never give
nature (or mankind) a final form, only a form that we must
distill until it is a "spirit": as good, true, and beautiful—and
nontoxic—as we can make it.

Levi began with a universe of rocks and men, but he did
not end with one. As he grew older, more and more organic
material lodged, survived, and flourished in the crevices and
outcroppings of those desolate peaks. He experienced love,
marriage, parenthood, career, adultery, fame, and many close
friendships. He enjoyed the simple aspects of life: eating and
drinking, walking in the mountains, playing chess with old
friends. His depression was tragic, but it was only part of his
organism, part of his life; and his late poems, while often sad,
also have a mellow ripeness, a fullness, appropriate for a man
who, although (or because) he never feels complete himself, is
as complete a man as we can imagine.

TEN

INTO THE SEA

P RIMO LEVI DIED April 11, 1987, after his most severe
episode of depression. His death was disturbing and mysterious: He fell over the third-floor balcony of an interior
stairwell in his apartment building. Most, but not all, commen-
tators have concluded that he took his own life. While the means
of death may seem unlikely, his grandfather committed suicide
in a nearly identical way, leaping from a second-story window in
1888. Moreover, Levi had at least twice referred to this form of
suicide. He had written in *If This Is a Man* that to catch diphthe-
ria in the Lager "was more surely fatal than jumping off a third
floor."[1] Also, Levi's lover, Gisella, in a diary entry from 1982–
1983, quotes him as saying: "This is the fourth depression of my
life. I want to end it. But the third floor is not high enough."[2]

Unlike his grandfather, who, because of his suicide, was
denied burial in the regular Jewish cemetery, Levi received a

normal burial because the Turin rabbi pronounced his death a case of "delayed murder" by the Nazis. This seems wrong: Levi's mental illness was not—in any obvious way—linked to his experiences at Auschwitz. Levi believed that some survivors killed themselves out of shame, but he also believed that he had written his way through that shame already. He had been upset by Holocaust deniers shortly before his death, but he had also been distressed by a surgical procedure he had undergone, the grinding burden of caring for his mother and mother-in-law, and the difficulty of writing *The Double Bond*. For all we know, Levi's depression had biochemical causes with little relation to life events. And, for all we know, Levi's death was accidental, or occurred in a zone between accident and intention that defies clear explanation. At a certain point, biographical speculation becomes fruitless.

Levi did not believe that the way a life—or any story—ended should determine its meaning. Ulysses, spared from so many shipwrecks, is in many ways the paradigmatic survivor, but he ends his life not as one of the saved but as one of the drowned. While this fact should complicate our feelings—and increase our respect—for those who drown, it should not convert Ulysses' whole life into the prologue to a drowning. Levi's magnificent "Canto of Ulysses" ends with Dante's line: "And over our heads the hollow seas closed up." But that last line, important as it is, hardly negates the ennobling encounter between Levi, Jean, Dante, and Ulysses that has just taken place.

The classic Levi tale ends in disaster, whether comic (the chemistry experiment goes awry), prophetic (the attempt to reengineer the species fails), or tragic (the prisoners are degraded and killed). Even a seemingly light memoir-story like "Argon" in *The Periodic Table* ends with a bad surprise: Levi's grandmother gives him a chocolate, but it is worm-ridden, and he hides it in his pocket with great embarrassment. But those endings are not *the* answer; they are not unmaskings of an ultimate reality. They may deepen and undermine the narratives that precede them, but they never simply cancel them.

Levi was still writing about Auschwitz and despair at the end of his life. One of his last essays was "The Black Hole of Auschwitz," which took issue with Holocaust deniers. His final newspaper article was "The Marital Web," a superficially whimsical piece that edges into despair as it describes female spiders that eat their mates after having sex. But in his last months Levi was also writing truly playful stories about giraffes, gulls, germs, and moles. He reviewed a new translation of his old favorite, *The Call of the Wild*. Jack London, Levi wrote, was a man who "fought to the bitter end for life and for survival, and drew from that battle his reason to write."[3] These last, far-ranging works remind us that, even as death was drawing near, Levi continued to fight, speculate, and even play.

Death is not determinative, but it certainly has an important, polyvalent place in Levi's work. In a poem from late 1984, called "Tasks Pending," Levi writes that he yearns to die quietly, without "disturbing the universe." He echoes J. Alfred Prufrock, who asks "Do I dare disturb the universe?" in T. S. Eliot's poem—which ends with the Levian image of reawakening only to drown. In the poem, Levi wants to leave like someone "slipping away from a feast." He recognizes that life has a banquet full of good things to offer, but they are no longer of interest to him. What bind him to life now are not pleasures, but duties: tasks, debts, and unbreakable commitments.[4] Only death can release him from obligations, but it would violate those obligations to die on purpose.

Levi wrote two death-haunted poems about crows. In "The Crow's Song," the crow is an external force speaking to Levi, but also Levi himself, speaking to his audience. Like the crow, Levi "came from very far away to bring bad news."[5] He came not to soothe us to sleep but to demand constant wakefulness, to remind us that evil and death are ever-present. In "The Crow's Song II," we hear nothing but the voice of the crow, an emissary of death, speaking to a man in terrifying terms. The crow has counted out the man's days, few and brief, filled with care and fear of death. It is useless to flee; the crow will follow you to the ends of the earth, your constant companion, until your strength dissolves and you die.[6]

In this poem, death is as brutal as the Auschwitz reveille that makes the heart crack in the breast. One never finds in Levi Walt Whitman's embrace of death as the great mother who rocks the cradle and causes mockingbirds to sing—or death as the magnificent ocean lapping our shores. More often, death is shipwreck, chaos, nothingness, extinction, and it is closely entangled with the Nazis, who sowed so much senseless death as to dissolve the old cosmos. Death is the alien command, the brutally ironic Wstawàch, "get up."

Levi's writings about suicide are complex and contradictory. In some essays, as in "On Obscure Writing," Levi seems to treat suicide as failure. But in other instances, Levi regards suicide scientifically: it is neither romantic nor taboo, but one among many natural responses to the world. In the story "Westward," a scientist studying lemmings discovers that they do not commit

suicide because they are hungry or overcrowded; they simply
do not want to live. He reports that humans, too, may be born
without the will to live, or they may lose it. And they are not
necessarily wrong to do so: "Life does *not* have a purpose," and
"pain always prevails over joy."[7] Nature has given us a will to
live, but it functions by covering up the truth, which is the
void.[8] Levi does not feel that life as a meaningless void is *the*
truth, but he certainly feels that it is *a* truth.

In an odd way, the availability of suicide is one of the things
that make life bearable. In *If This Is a Man* Levi comments on
the fact that in the most desperate circumstances one always
has the sense of being lucky:

> Strange, how in some way one always has the impression of
> being fortunate, how some chance happening, perhaps infini-
> tesimal, stops us crossing the threshold of despair and allows
> us to live. It is raining, but it is not windy. Or else, it is raining
> and also windy: but you know that this evening it is your turn
> for the supplement of soup, so that even today you find the
> strength to reach the evening. Or it is raining, windy and you
> have the usual hunger, and then you think that if you really
> had to, if you really felt nothing in your heart but suffering and
> tedium—as sometimes happens, when you really seem to lie
> on the bottom,—well, even in that case, at any moment you
> want you could always go and touch the electric wire-fence,
> or throw yourself under the shunting trains, and then it would
> stop raining.[9]

Suicide, in this passage, is a perfectly rational response to
suffering and tedium, to lying on the bottom, shipwrecked.
Moreover, man's ability to take his own life is part of his dignity, what makes him a man; as Levi says in *If This Is a Man,*

when he is suffering the death-in-life of Auschwitz, "I am not even alive enough to know how to kill myself."[10] Suicide, he writes in *The Drowned and the Saved,* is the act of a man and not of an animal; it is a meditated, noninstinctive, unnatural choice—one that became unavailable at Auschwitz precisely because men had been reduced to animals.[11]

Life ends in death, and sometimes even in the desire for death, the black hole, but that is not the whole story. In the 1978 poem "Pliny," Levi offers quite a different view, in which death is both more human and more natural. Pliny was the Roman historian and scientist who was asphyxiated by toxic fumes when he went too close to Mount Vesuvius in an attempt to study its great eruption. The poem is loosely based on a famous letter by Pliny's nephew describing his uncle's last hours. Pliny addresses his friends, asking them not to hold him back. They need not fear the volcano's ash; after all, we are ash ourselves. They should let him go to study the phenomena and record it in books. He ends his speech, and the poem, with the wonderful exhortation: "Sailors, obey me: launch the boat into the sea."[12]

Reading this, one thinks of Dante's Canto of Ulysses and the importance Levi placed, in remembering it at Auschwitz, on "setting forth" and "venturing" on the open sea.[13] Like Ulysses, Pliny is making a great speech before setting out on a doomed quest for knowledge and excellence. What will happen to Pliny after he dies? Levi does not believe that Pliny will go to hell, like Dante's Ulysses. Nor does he believe that Pliny will vanish into a black hole. Pliny is allowed the hope that his books will still live (and, in fact, they do survive as literature, even though the science in them has been proven false). Even for Pliny's body there is another possibility, beyond "whirling dissolved in the cosmic vortices": his atoms may live again in an "eagle, a young girl, a flower."[14] Organic chemistry, nature, has its own modes of survival and renewal, its own ways of reusing ash, its own forms of change beyond entropy, its own way of saving those that drown.

ELEVEN

WHAT WE MAKE OF
EACH OTHER

P RIMO LEVI WANTED to create a cosmos, an interpretation of the world, along with an ethos, a coherent view
of how to live. And yet he vehemently rejected the role
of a guru, telling an interviewer that prophets are the curse of
our time, and perhaps of all time.[1] In his essay "The Eclipse of
the Prophets," Levi argues that no ultimate authority is possible, and that to believe in one is to succumb to idol worship.
We are orphans, he writes, and we must live with the malaise
of orphans. The human condition is incompatible with certainty.[2]

Every decalogue, no matter how well made, no matter how
individualized, is suspect. Levi's norms do not always work,
even for himself. As he says in *The Search for Roots*, introducing

Stefano D'Arrigo's *Horcynus Orca*—a work he loves, despite the way it violates all his rules:

> You are constructing your own private decalogue (work in progress, but you have the illusion of having done it already). Your writing shall be concise, clear, composed; you will avoid whatever is willed and over-elaborated...Then you come across *Horcynus Orca* and everything flies out the window.[3]

Levi believes not just in salvation through understanding, but also in salvation through laughter: laughter that expresses an exuberant love of life and an ironic, doubting attitude toward systems and ideologies. In *The Search for Roots,* he writes that, when it comes to authors, he prefers the magicians to the moralists.

Levi does not believe in grand revelations, in booming voices from the clouds. He prefers to work for what he calls "more modest and less exciting truths" of the sort that are won with hard work, bit by bit, with no cut corners, through study, discussion, reasoning, which can then be checked and shown to be true.[4] In contrast to many scientists and philosophers, Levi includes discussion as an integral part of truth seeking. Much as he loves Odysseus, he loves him more as a conversationalist than as a warrior king. In the essay "Thirty Hours on *Castoro Sei*," when he is praising the crew of a submarine by comparing them to Odysseus, he says:

> ...in their controlled, educated, precise, and unrhetorical words, I have recognized the echo of the voice of another navigator and storyteller whose remote adventures are today eternal poetry: the navigator who journeyed for ten years across strange seas and whose prime virtues, much more than

courage, which he had in abundance, were patience and mul-
tifarious ingenuity.[5]

Only Levi would hear echoes of Odysseus in "controlled, educated, precise, and unrhetorical" words. But of course Levi *is* a
controlled, educated, precise, and unrhetorical Odysseus.

Real understanding is a democratic, mutual process. What
we make of ourselves is inextricable from what we make of
each other. The listening is as important as the telling, and one
of Levi's chief tasks is to teach us his form of active, engaged
listening. As he writes in *The Monkey's Wrench,* "[j]ust as there
is an art of storytelling, strictly codified through a thousand
trials and errors, so there is also an art of listening, equally
ancient and noble, but as far as I know, it has never been given
any norm."[6] In *If This Is a Man*, he says that a major torment in
Auschwitz was the fact that no one had the time and patience
to listen. His recurring nightmare in the Lager was not of torture or death: it was of coming home and recounting his experience to indifferent listeners. Levi was a good listener, which
is one of the reasons he formed so many close friendships and
why he heard so many good stories over the years; as he writes
in *The Periodic Table*, "I am one of those people to whom many
things are told."[7]

Levi learned how to listen in many languages. He learned
French well enough to translate Levi-Strauss, German well
enough to translate Kafka, English well enough to translate
Mary Douglas, and Yiddish well enough to attempt to repro-
duce its inflections in *If Not Now, When?*. It was as if he were
personally undoing the Babel that the Nazis had created in the
camps, raveling the languages back together into mutual com-
municability. He disliked theories of incommunicability: as he

writes in *The Drowned and the Saved*, "one can and must communicate...one always can."[8]

But communication is far from an unambiguous good. There are times for discretion and silence. As Levi writes in *If This Is a Man,* "Few know how to remain silent and respect the silence of others."[9] Speech is not a universal solvent. Moreover, it can be corrupted at any time. Levi once proposed, in an interview with Ferdinando Camon, that communication was at the essence of the extraordinary rise of Nazism:

> In my opinion, the means was propaganda. It's the first case in history in which an especially powerful and violent man, a tyrant, found himself in possession of the spectacular weapon of mass communications. Mussolini, as an organizer of huge rallies, had put on a good show, but Hitler outdid him ten- or twenty-fold...When hundreds of thousands shouted "We swear!" in one voice, it was as though they'd become a single body.[10]

The communication Levi prized was not mass communication but conversation, which was for him a kind of communion, because "part of our existence lies in the feelings of those near to us."[11] He was a master of reasoned conversation, so much so that his interviews should be read as a core part of his literary work (more central, perhaps, than his novels). He believed in face-to-face contact as equals: in *The Drowned and the Saved,* he writes that there are no problems that cannot be solved around a table with good will and trust.[12]

Much of Levi's work has a conversational style. In one of his last pieces, "To Our Generation," he describes it as "a kind of uninterrupted dialogue with my readers."[13] *If This Is a Man* originated in his compulsive telling of his Auschwitz tales to relatives, friends, and even near-strangers after his return to Turin. Like his other writings, it creates an unusually intense relationship between author and reader. On the third page, he tells how the Jews of the internment camp at Fossoli prepared for their deportation to Auschwitz, the mothers carefully washing the children's clothes and packing up their toys and cushions. And then he asks, "Would you not do the same? If you and your child were going to be killed tomorrow, would you not give him to eat today?"[14] Levi relates to the reader as he relates to Jean the Pikolo in "The Canto of Ulysses" when he says, "Here, listen Pikolo, open your ears and your mind, you have to understand, for my sake."[15]

Levi cared deeply about the reception of his work; he was not a man who wrote for himself. He kept a log of all his reviews, writing down the name of the reviewer, title of the periodical, and marks from one to five in two columns: one mark reflecting how the reviewer judged him, and one mark reflecting how he judged the reviewer.[16] At the end of his life, when a bizarrely aggressive review appeared in *Commentary*, he described it as absolutely crippling and wrote to his translator, "It is not merely for this episode that I have lost my good humor and the will to live."[17] Levi demands, for many reasons, most of all his greatness and his complexity, to be read with care. As he told an interviewer, a good book must be polyvalent.[18] Any conclusions must be tentative.

"What do we make of each other?" is one way to phrase the question Levi poses in all of his writings and interviews. In *If This Is a Man*, Dr. Pannwitz does not try to understand Levi; he uses him like a machine part, as Alex the Kapo uses him for a rag. Jean the Pikolo, by contrast, tries to understand what Levi is saying—to learn his language—and thus restores Levi's humanity. In an interview, Levi says that he married Lucia in part because she listened better, more deeply, to him and his tales of Auschwitz than anyone else; she knew, or intuited, what to make of him.[19]

Understanding another person means, in part, recognizing that one can never fully understand him or her. Levi writes in his essay "Jean Améry, Philosopher and Suicide":

> [E]ach and every human action contains a kernel of incomprehensibility. If this were not the case, we would be in a position to foresee what our neighbor is going to do. Clearly we cannot do this, and perhaps it is just as well that we cannot.[20]

Thinking that one completely understands another is an act of hubris, comparable to the attempt to create a human being from scratch. Many of Levi's fables concern failed efforts to create, replicate, or improve human creatures. In the story "The Hard Sellers," Levi describes a soul named S. waiting to be incarnated on Earth. S. rejects the ready-made life of privilege being offered by the experts and demands the chance to create himself:

> I prefer to be born black, Indian, poor, without indulgences and without pardons. . . . You yourself said that each man is his own maker: well, it is best to be so fully, build oneself from the roots. I prefer to be the only one to fabricate myself, and I prefer the anger that I will need if I will be capable of it . . .[21]

But in Levi's best work, self-creation is not the solitary affair S. suggests, but rather a mutual process among equals. Hence the importance of friends in Levi's memoirs, the importance of loving and being loved—which makes his universe, for all its metaphysical bleakness, seem richer and more human than the worlds, for example, of *Moby Dick* or *Heart of Darkness*.

In the very late poem entitled "To My Friends," Levi addresses his friends in the most generous sense of the word: his wife, sister, associates, relatives, schoolmates, even people he has seen only once—provided that, at least for a moment, a line connected them, a "well-defined chord." Tellingly, Levi includes even the shipwrecked, those who have lost their souls or their desire to live. He asks these friends to remember the time "Before the wax hardened, / When each of us was like a seal"—being stamped by one another.[22]

Levi prized the period in life before the wax hardens: when we are capable of reason yet still susceptible to change, to the influence of friends and teachers. That is why he loved Conrad's *Youth* and why his best writing centered on his own youth. That is why he confessed to a certain paradoxical nostalgia for Auschwitz, because, as he told an interviewer, "the Lager coincided with my youth, and it is for my youth, and for the few people with whom I made friends at Auschwitz, that I feel nostalgia."[23] That is why he was willing to make so many appearances at schools in Italy: the formation of souls was at stake. Very few Nazis were sadistic monsters; most of them were, he says, simply products of their education.[24]

The moments when we connect with each other are moments of reprieve, not just enjoyable but also enlightening, moments when the random black matter of the universe condenses not into a black hole, but into a small light that we can see by. For this, books are good but not sufficient; they lack sufficient mutuality. At Auschwitz, if Levi had remembered Dante in a moment of solitude, it would not have meant as much; but to speak about Dante with Jean was vital and nourishing. Levi does believe in the sacred; however, he finds it not in theology but in the relation of man to man. He writes in "The Black Hole of Auschwitz" that "man is, must be, sacred to man, everywhere and forever."[25]

The fact that we are what we make of each other also explains the urgency of language and communication in Levi's work. Levi stopped visiting schools, he said, because he feared that his language had become inadequate, outdated.[26] And, in describing Auschwitz, he said, "I felt it like a burning brand, like a form of torture, being in a world whose words, whose language was incomprehensible, where we could not make ourselves understood."[27] The Polish spoken in the camps was even more of a torment than German because Levi knew almost none of it; it was the language of the void.

As Levi explained in interviews, the failure of communication was a central feature of Auschwitz because "an abyss divides the person who can make himself understood from the person who cannot: one is saved and the other is lost."[28] In the most practical terms, inability to understand German was generally lethal in the Lager; it doomed most of the Italian Jews within the first weeks.[29] In broader terms, Levi cannot conceive of a meaningful life without communication. Thus the passion with which, in *The Truce*, he portrays the struggle of Hurbinek, the three-year-old boy from Auschwitz struggling to say a word:

> Hurbinek continued in his stubborn experiments for as long as he lived. In the following days everybody listened to him

in silence, anxious to understand, and among us there were speakers of all the languages of Europe; but Hurbinek's word remained secret. No, it was certainly not a message, it was not a revelation; perhaps it was his name, if it had ever fallen to his lot to be given a name....

Hurbinek, who was three years old and perhaps had been born in Auschwitz and had never seen a tree; Hurbinek, who had fought like a man, to the last breath, to gain his entry into the world of men, from which a bestial power had excluded him; Hurbinek, the nameless, whose tiny forearm—even his— bore the tattoo of Auschwitz; Hurbinek died in the first days of March 1945, free but not redeemed. Nothing remains of him: he bears witness through these words of mine.[30]

The final sentence encapsulates Hurbinek's paradoxical existence and death. Nothing remains of him—he loses his fight to snatch language out of the jaws of death—and yet, through his power to bear suffering and survive, at least for a while, he does "bear" something; or, at least, he impregnates Levi with a memory that gives birth to Levi's words and grants tiny Hurbinek immortality: what Levi calls, in *Moments of Reprieve,* the "ambiguous perennial existence of a literary character."[31]

Levi's lifelong disgust for violence is closely related to his affirmation of discourse, particularly reasoned discourse, as the essence of humanity. It is no accident that, in *The Drowned and the Saved*, the chapter "Communicating" is followed by the chapter "Useless Violence." In Auschwitz, kicks, slaps, and punches are the language—or anti-language—because the inmates and guards have been reduced to beasts. Levi resorts to violence only once, when Elias pushes him up against the wall and bawls insults in his face; Levi kicks him in the shins, conscious of betraying himself. Other than this one experience, Levi tells us that he has lived his whole life without "trading punches."[32] He feels incapable of personal vengeance, preferring to delegate the role of punishment to the law, however inadequate it is. As he writes in the afterword to *If This Is a Man:*

> I believe in reason and in discussion as supreme instruments of progress, and therefore I repress hatred even within myself: I prefer justice. Precisely for this reason, when describing the tragic world of Auschwitz, I have deliberately assumed the calm, sober language of the witness, neither the lamenting tones of the victim nor the irate voice of someone who seeks revenge. I thought that my account would be all the more credible and useful the more it appeared objective and the less it sounded overly emotional; only in this way does a witness in matters of justice perform his task, which is that of preparing the ground for the judge. The judges are my readers.[33]

No one can deconstruct Levi's writing as well as Levi. In presenting himself as the sober witness, he adds a layer of irony by saying that he "deliberately assumed" his calm language because he thought it would be more credible, the more it "appeared" objective.

While always careful to maintain his irony, his sense of the limits of language, Levi cannot quite rest with George Steiner's conclusion that "the world of Auschwitz lies outside speech as it lies outside reason."[34] In *If This Is a Man* he claims that our language lacks the words to express the demolition of a man, but then he does find words to express it, to bring it into the light of understanding.[35] Even if the task is impossible, it remains essential. As he writes in *The Search for Roots* in the introduction to his excerpt from Job:

> Why start with Job? Because this magnificent and harrowing story encapsulates the questions of all the ages, those for which man has never to this day found an answer, nor will he ever find one, but he will always search for it because he needs it in order to live, to understand himself and the world.[36]

We are in a double bind: we have to search for an understanding that we need in order to live and yet will never find. At a certain point, then, we may give up, but, in the meantime, what we will we do, how will we behave, what less-than-ultimate but still real understanding will we gain?

Complete understanding is not even desirable. One should not try to fully understand the Nazis because that would come too close to justifying them. Moreover, most understanding involves a degree of simplification. Conceptual thought is necessary for orienting ourselves and making decisions in the tangled world, but it is inevitably reductive and therefore false.[37] Humans, in particular, cannot be reduced to words: as a character in "Bear Meat" says, "it's a desperate endeavor to clothe a man in words."[38]

While he was drafting *If This Is a Man*, Levi also wrote a story called "The Mnemogogues." In it he depicts a provincial doctor named Montesanto, who has found a way to synthesize the scents that arouse meaningful memories for him, an occupation much like Levi's distilling of his own memories into art. Montesanto, like Levi, has suffered through an aborted university career and a cruel initiation in the war.

Now he has ended up a municipal doctor in a forsaken town, searching for something "too indefinable to ever be found."[39] Montesanto describes his life as a lonely man amidst small, lighthearted people, and he tells the narrator about "the definite prevalence of the past over the present, and the final shipwreck of every passion, except for his faith in the dignity of thought and the supremacy of the things of the spirit."[40] In Levi's life story, as in Montesanto's, many things are shipwrecked, and many people are drowned, but the dignity of thought and the supremacy of the things of the spirit are saved.

Levi never lets the black holes have the last word; he continues until the very end—writing, right before his death, "The Black Hole of Auschwitz"—to oppose reasoned discourse to chaos and violence. He never minimizes the terror of the black holes, but, in applying reason to them, he finds consolation. One may think meaningfully about both kinds of black holes, the human and the astronomical. In *The Search for Roots,* he writes:

> Every year that passes, while earthly matters grow ever more convoluted, the challenge of the cosmos grows keener and more bitter: the heavens are not simple, but neither are they impenetrable to our minds—they are waiting to be deciphered. The misery of man has another face, one imprinted with nobility; maybe we exist by chance, perhaps we are the sole instance of intelligence in the universe, certainly, we are immeasurably small, weak and alone, but if the human mind has conceived Black Holes, and dares to speculate on what happened in the first moments of creation, why should it not know how to conquer fear, poverty, and grief?[41]

We must remain vigilant; we must continue to reason in the face of all our failures. As Levi tells an interviewer:

> To believe in reason means believing in your own reason, it doesn't mean that reason rules the world nor even that it governs man. To have been present at the shipwreck of reason—and here I'm referring not only to Nazism, but also to our own Fascism—must not and cannot lead us to surrender...for our generation there is no respite. For reason too there is no respite, we cannot take a holiday from reason.[42]

Levi does not believe in the supernatural. He does not believe that men can become angels, before or after death. The goal, therefore, is not to transcend humanity. The goal is to avoid devolution into beasts: to forge a humanity worthy of the name.

The Italian publisher Einaudi had two famous authors named Levi: one was Primo, and the other one was Carlo Levi, the author of *Christ Stopped at Eboli*. To distinguish them, the staff called Carlo *Levi Cristo* and Primo *Levi Uomo*. All his life, Levi tried to be *Levi Uomo*. He said late in life, "Yes, I suppose I've wanted that too, without achieving it—to be, myself, *un uomo completo*."[43] To become and remain a man is an achievement, an arduous and incessant battle, the outcome of which is never guaranteed. As Levi said, "Since there is a very real risk of ruin, the only remedy is to roll up our sleeves."[44] And struggle, as he did, so patiently and beautifully, for illumination.

AFTERWORD

THERE WAS A time, not too long ago, when Primo Levi was not yet *Primo Levi*. At the beginning of his writing life, he was appreciated by a group of aficionados, but if he was recognized outside those circles, he was known as something of a niche author. The aficionados were first his friends—many of them Jews from Turin—plus his mother, sister, wife, and cousins. His first book, the now-classic *Se questo è un uomo*, was met with stony indifference from the general public and critics alike (though budding author Italo Calvino wrote one positive, prescient review). Only much later did the Italian literary community cautiously hail him by awarding him, in 1963, the first Campiello Prize. But it also snubbed him because he was a scientist, a varnish maker, an outsider (the great Mario Rigoni Stern, similarly derided by the Italian literary establishment, became Levi's fast friend). Levi was judged a fleeting phenomenon, a flash-in-the-pan.

Then acclaim came anew in the 1980s, this time louder, more lasting, and from abroad. The English-speaking world rushed to praise *Il sistema periodico,* published as *The Periodic Table.* The Italian literary establishment, the insular gatekeepers of fine culture—trained in the classics, with editorships at premier publishing houses and university sinecures, all regulars at the literary salons—was again surprised and, this time, compelled to take notice. Famous abroad? Perhaps some enduring talent had been overlooked?

The extra burst of activity that Levi experienced after his 1975 retirement bore fruit in that decade: poetry, novels, memoirs, an avalanche of op-ed writing, public pronouncements, position papers, and their translations into the world's major languages characterized the writer in his sixties. Levi received the unexpected warm embrace of America's literary lions (Roth and Howe, foremost among them). In 1984, one of his less-read books, *Se non ora, quando?* (*If Not Now, When?*), became a U.S. sensation. Like a far-off supernova, it pointed back to Levi's origins in a parallel universe, the *univers concentrationnaire,* and led readers to his early works, *If This Is a Man,* in particular. Eager to know more, readers sought out his other works, just as Levi was about to publish his summa, *I sommersi e i salvati* (*The Drowned and the Saved*). Levi rapidly—improbably, for an author perceived to be at the fringes of the literary establishment, and an Italian perceived to be at the fringes of the Jewish world—became the face of Italian Jewry and the voice of Holocaust testimony, wherever its geographic point of origin. His thought was pure and piercing, his constructions apparently guileless and communicative, such that his intrinsically Italian narrative rang universal for many.

Then, his premature death.

Biographers on two continents turned their attention to Primo Levi beginning in 1996 and, over the course of the next six years, produced three massive tomes totaling over 2,100 pages. And yet, as *Primo Levi's Universe* shows, Levi's story still benefits from the (re)telling, much as viewing a supernova can benefit from different vantage points. Sam Magavern brings a fresh sensibility to the genre and produces—something Levi might have appreciated—a hybrid book, part life story and part literary study. The watchwords of Magavern's process are reflection, restraint, and a deep reading of Levi's works—most fruitfully, and refreshingly, of his later poetry and essays.

Magavern suggests that a key to Levi's life is not his biography but his works. A focus on the hodgepodge of details in Levi's life actually undercuts his value and weight. Scholars (like me, I confess) may crave the minutiae, and we've been amply rewarded by previous efforts. What Levi's readers may want, instead, is a book, like this one, that explores and explains how the "civilian" Primo Levi became Primo Levi the author we know today. In other words, how Primo Levi—through intense reflection and study, force of will and habit, and potentially painful rumination—created and defined his post-Auschwitz existence. In *Primo Levi's Universe*, Magavern dissects Levi's life not as biography but as bildungsroman and exposes the steps of Levi's self-making.

I had a brief acquaintanceship with Primo Levi, lasting but a few hours, when I was a student and he was near the top of the fame he achieved in his lifetime. I had been warned that meetings with celebrities inevitably fail to meet expectations but in this instance I was not disappointed. Quite the opposite: interviewing him had lasting effects and cast him as a polestar for my professional and scholarly life.

In 1984, while living in Florence, I had discovered Levi through a *New York Times* review of *The Periodic Table*. I was astonished and chagrined, as an American Jew in Italy, that I had never heard of the man whom the *Times* reviewer, John Gross, pronounced a great Italian author. I promptly began to read Levi's books, beginning with the first, *If This Is a Man*.

The following year, I found myself in graduate school in Massachusetts and searching for a thesis topic. I thought of the books of Levi's I had devoured and was still reading outside my course work. Might Primo Levi be a suitable academic subject? It is difficult to reconcile Levi's current fame with the advice I was given at the time, i.e., that Levi might be a man with a compelling life story but he was not an "author," that he was far outside the literary canon, and that the enduring value of his books was unproven and might remain so. Undeterred (or just green), I determined to write on Levi nonetheless, but my advisers' view was only reinforced during a funding search. American Jewish organizations pronounced Levi and Italy— unlike Eastern Europe, Israel, or the large Western European Jewish communities in France and Germany—outside of their purviews, and Italian-American funding organizations replied that Holocaust studies and Italian Jewish writers were marginal to their mandates. In 1985, Levi seemed to live in a no-man's land, not Jewish enough, not Italian enough, not author enough.

Shortly thereafter, through a six-degrees-of-separation chain of events, I serendipitously found myself in Turin at Levi's doorstep. When the author himself opened the door to his apartment on Corso Re Umberto on June 19, 1986, and led me into his sitting room, all the trepidation I had felt on meeting a famous author dissolved. He was a small man, with a shock of white hair receding to just the right authorial degree. His inquisitive glance and easy laugh made the tone of our conversation pleasant, though the content was serious.

After a half hour, Levi got up to prepare a *caffé*, and I had time to take in my surroundings. The living room of his fourth-floor apartment was furnished with the sort of *fin-de-siècle* chairs and sofas and cool stone tiles one would expect to find in the parlor of one's great aunt. Levi, in fact, had been born in that very apartment, in 1919, and it had been in the family for many years. The pictures on the wall, the small statues on the tables, the color of the furniture were all unobtrusive. (Levi confessed, somewhat embarrassed, that several of the statues were *fantasie* he had made himself.) My attention was drawn to Levi's desk, the double window, and the two massive bookcases behind the desk. One bookcase was devoted entirely to Holocaust-related writings in all the modern European languages (including Yiddish and Hebrew). The other had a shelf on which Levi kept his favorite books, dog-eared and annotated. He indicated that he kept them arranged not chronologically or alphabetically, but in order of importance. I've since berated myself many times for not having taken a photograph of the books on that shelf. Some twenty years later, are those books still arranged in the same order? The one incongruous element in Levi's living room was the word processor on Levi's desk, plastic as opposed to the wood, stone, and linen of the rest of the house. Huge by today's standards, it formed a boxy barrier between the scholar's corner and his gracious apartment.

Levi came back in shirtsleeves and carrying a tray with coffee, and we talked for the next three hours. Before that day, I had never read an interview with Levi and knew nothing about him as a person other than what could be gleaned from his books. I did not know that some of the same questions I asked had been put to him many times before. He never let on that he had already answered these questions; instead, he remained patient, kindly, and remarkably serene. The atmosphere in his living room was peaceful, despite the fact that the topics we discussed were often painful—not only the Holocaust, but his family life, too. I felt that something special for me and perhaps unusual for Levi transpired in this exchange. Later, as I read earlier interviews with Levi, I realized that our conversation took place on a private, personal plane that most professional interviews lacked.

As I was preparing for the interview, Levi's book *The Drowned and the Saved* was published. The *summa* of his thoughts on the Shoah, on memory, communication, and "useless violence" in the Lager, and—most memorably— his postulation of the "grey zone"—it formed the backbone for the questions I asked. But the conversation also moved into personal territory, a rarity in Levi's interviews. I first asked Levi whether he considered himself a "Jewish writer," to which he replied with surprise, and some lingering acrimony, that the American Jews had first pinned that identity on him, with Italians instead considering him "a writer who is occasionally Jewish."[1] He spoke of his close relationship to the Jewish community of Turin (he was active in community governance, and wrote a warm preface to the community-sponsored 1984 volume *Ebrei a Torino*). At the same time, he stated categorically, "I am not a believer."

Levi also expressed unexpectedly harsh views of psychoanalysis, despite a lifelong depressive tendency and repeated periods of crisis. When I remarked that he seemed "a bit hostile toward psychoanalysis," he replied, "In fact, I am! Psychoanalysts today leave me cold. They're schematic. Mind you, I'm not psychotic myself and I've never had any direct experience!" This last denial appears disingenuous: it is true that Levi was not psychotic, but he did receive mental health treatment, took antidepressants, and counted among his oldest and closest friends Luciana Nissim, an Auschwitz survivor and, later, a psychoanalyst in Milan.

Levi spoke at length of the need to bear witness and the quality of his memories. In that context, he again touched on psychoanalysis, though the tone was different: "I really needed to tell [my story . . .] I had the feeling that I think Catholics must have when they go to confession: it's a great relief to confess. Or the feeling you have if you're in therapy with a psychoanalyst, and by telling your story you break free of it." Continuing, he commented, "But there's more to it than that. A very intelligent friend of mine once said to me, 'That period was in Technicolor and the rest of your life has been in black and white.' And that's pretty close to the truth."

I asked him several times about how he became a writer. Initially, he answered, "First of all, as I've already said—and honestly must say—writing was a liberating act. I had these things inside of me and I had to get them out. But at the same time, it was also very political." Would *The Drowned and the*

Saved be his last Auschwitz book? "I grew up at Auschwitz," he replied. "I don't know if it's a virtue, or fortune, or something else, but I truly accumulated an enormous amount of material, of notions, of considerations that I have yet to fully sort out." And would he have been a writer without having been to Auschwitz? Levi bristled at first. "Not only have I asked myself that question, but everyone else asks me that too. I don't know how to answer. It's as if I asked you, 'If you hadn't been born in America, what would you do?' You can't answer that." After I insisted, he replied,

> I don't know, but I can make some suppositions. I probably wouldn't have taken up writing, or I would have written who knows what. I was a chemist beforehand—by conviction, mind you! In fact, I worked as a chemist all my life. I think I can take as examples some of my friends who didn't go to Auschwitz and who tranquilly continued in their professions. They started families. I started a family, too; I got married and I had children. If I hadn't gone to Auschwitz, I probably wouldn't have written, or I would have written completely different things—maybe scholarly articles about chemistry. I certainly possessed the capacity to write, I can't deny that. I wasn't born of nothing: I had received a fairly rigid classical education and I already possessed the faculty to write. But I wouldn't have had—how can I explain it?—the "raw material" to become a writer.

With unblinking self-awareness and a willingness to divulge the indelicate, Levi acknowledges the irony that his later success was predicated on his most ignominious moment.

Magavern and others make a strong case that it is the very literary calculus that went into writing *If This Is a Man*—the

analogies, the composite portraits, the finely calibrated characters, the literary and Biblical references, the incisive phrases—
that have fixed it in the public consciousness and account for
its fame. Yet when I asked Levi whether he concentrated on
style when writing his books, he answered, "Now I do; when
I wrote *If This Is a Man* I didn't [...] At that time, I didn't pay
any attention to style. I wrote *If This Is a Man* without giving it
a second thought: at night, in the lab, on the train, wherever I
happened to find myself." Then, with a twinkle in his eye, he
added, "But I didn't have much time then—I was also engaged
to be married!"

At that point, our conversation veered toward the personal.
Levi spoke of the intense conflict he felt between his current
family duties and his growing international fame. The latter
led to invitations to speak around the world—invitations that
delighted him yet that he felt compelled to refuse, due to his
home situation.

> Let me tell you, my wife and I are in a disastrous state here in
> Italy. We have two people to take care of: My mother is 91 (she's
> in the next room); my mother-in-law is 95 and blind. We can't
> go anywhere because even though we have help, they go on
> vacation in the summer. So for us, instead of being a break, the
> summer is always a problem. Although I was invited to go to the
> United States in November [1986], when *The Monkey's Wrench*
> is scheduled to appear, I wrote that I wouldn't be able to accept.
> If I go, I leave the whole burden on my wife's shoulders. By a
> miracle, we were able to get away for twelve or thirteen days in
> April, but only by asking my sister to come up from Rome, and
> she also has her own burdens. We can't go anywhere. I've done
> nothing but turn down invitations right and left.

Levi looked quite stricken and, instinctively, I tried to cheer him up—to no avail, as it turned out. I said, "Your mother and mother-in-law are very long-lived." Levi replied,

My mother-in-law is 95, but she has two sisters in the United States: One is 97, and the other is 96. The youngest lives here and she is 89. It's a strangely long-lived family."

"That bodes well for you!" I said, to which Levi replied,

It depends on how you age. My mother-in-law is blind. She's been completely blind for fifteen years. We really need some-one around the clock. My mother isn't blind, but she's very senile. We have to do everything for her as well. As a result, I can't make any plans. In fact, my plans are not to make plans. I can only write. I've had invitations from everywhere. I had an invitation to go to Germany. I am very interested because a German editor has just signed a contract to republish all my books in their entirety. Discussions with the Germans could be very interesting. But for now I've said no. Then I've had the invitation to go to the United States in November....

In fact, last year, I was there but I came away half mad. I gave twenty-five interviews in twenty days—and I don't speak English that well. Well, I speak it well enough, but I under-stand it very poorly. Twenty-five interviews, six conferences and nine flights. I was in six cities. Everything was in a hurry. And I'm no longer a young man. Then back at the hotel, we had to keep the phone off the hook because otherwise we would get phone calls at all hours of the night—pleasant ones, to be sure, but it was impossible to rest."

I suddenly was moved by Levi's predicament and blurted out, "If you want to remain anonymous, you can stay at my house!" Levi replied with a wry smile, "Thank you, but if I come to America, it's because I'm not anonymous."

Lesson learned.

I've thought back to that part of the interview countless times since Levi's death just ten months later, on April 11, 1987. He expressed an untenable predicament. The intense conflict between his duties at home and his life outside the home is one that many ordinary people share. Far from the bravado of a literary superstar, Levi expressed the struggles of the common man. With this in mind, in the days after his death I especially recoiled from the hasty linking of Levi's suicide to his Holocaust experience. In life, Levi had managed to turn that terrible experience into something of value: a font of information, memories, types, and sociological knowledge. It was "in Technicolor" and the rest of his life "in black and white" (the opposite visual analogy to Steven Spielberg's *Schindler's List*, the Holocaust film shot in black-and-white, or Roberto Benigni's *Life Is Beautiful*, the popular "Holocaust fable" shot in color but with a muted palette in the concentration camp scenes). Yet headlines at the time trumpeted Levi's death as a tragedy that could and should be read as a direct consequence of the Holocaust.

I am also mindful of Levi's words and demeanor on that June 1986 day—calm and analytical while speaking about Auschwitz, troubled when speaking about his private life. Magavern cautions against linking Levi's depressive states to his experiences at Auschwitz: the causes may have been "biochemical." Perhaps even genetic causes were to blame: Levi's grandfather committed suicide nearly 100 years earlier, in 1888, by leaping from a second-story window. As Magavern concludes, "at a certain point further biographical speculation becomes fruitless."[2]

A most extraordinary meditation on Levi's life was published last year in France: *Il m'appelait Pikolo: Un compagnon de Primo Levi raconte* (He called me Pikolo: a campmate of Primo Levi recounts). In this memoir, Jean Samuel, the "Pikolo" of the Ulysses chapter of *If This Is a Man*, casts his entire life story in the shadow of his friendship with Primo Levi. Of the many *exempla* scattered through Levi's first book, few are as searing and memorable as the portrait of Pikolo in "The Canto of Ulysses."

Levi and Pikolo, together with fellow campmates Charles (Conreau) and Alberto (Dalla Volta), formed a rare sodality in the Lager. In a universe where names were usurped by numbers, and where lack of companionship often equaled death, Magavern comments that Pikolo is the first person in *If This Is a Man* to call Levi by name.[3] It is quite astonishing, then— and sobering—to read Samuel's revelation that, in their post-Auschwitz correspondence, the two men signed their letters, respectively, "Pikolo, ex 176,397" and "Primo, ex 174,517." It was as if their tattoo numbers had indelibly altered their identity as men, as if the former Jean Samuel and the former Primo Levi had been subsumed by a new identity that would forever both incorporate Auschwitz (via their tattoo numbers) and repudiate it (via the prefix "ex"). Samuel analyzes those signatures thus: "Very often, we signed out letters with our matriculation numbers preceded by the word 'ex,' to show clearly that we were no longer in the camp, but also that what we had lived through could never be erased."[4]

Samuel further reveals that the term "Pikolo" which, when read in the context of *If This Is a Man*, is presented as much a Nazi-generated administrative title as *Kesselwäscher* (vatwasher) or *Bademeister* (shower superintendent), was instead "invented for me by Primo Levi. I was the only Pikolo," he writes.[5]

Another surprise awaits us, as Samuel recounts a story that may be familiar in its details but whose cast in this telling is unfamiliar: it is the story of Alex the Kapo. Levi had written in *If This Is a Man* that Alex the guard had wiped his greasy hand on Levi's shoulder, thus reducing Levi to a rag, a mere thing, a non-man. That small offense assumes massive proportions for Levi, and he writes, "he would be amazed, the poor brute Alex, if someone told him today, on the basis of this action, I judge him and Pannwitz and the innumerable others like him, big and small, in Auschwitz and everywhere."[6] Samuel also tells the story but, in his version, he is the human rag, not Levi.

> In May or June, there was the question of recruiting chemists to work in a laboratory. I stepped forward as a candidate. The *Kapo* brought me and other prisoners (I no longer remember how many of us there were) to a factory building inside which was the office of the engineers responsible for the polymerization project. At that instant, when the *Kapo* came out of the room, I felt his hand on my clothes. But his gesture wasn't addressed toward me. He was neither attaching me nor comforting me: he was merely cleaning his hand, without even looking at me. I was nothing but a rag that he happened to find there at the exact moment that he had sullied his fingers. Even

today, recounting that scene, I feel the same humiliation I felt at the time.[7]

Perhaps it is another example of Levi recasting the facts to fit his purpose, as Magavern explores in the chapter "Uncertain Hours."

In Samuel's last chapter, "L'adieu à Primo" (Farewell to Primo), he attempts to come to terms with Levi's death. "There has been much speculation," he writes, "about the reasons for his death: was it or was it not a suicide by throwing himself down the stairwell? I have no certainty." He continues by commenting on the physical makeup of that stairwell, noting that the railing was very low and that one might easily topple over into the void. This same detail is the primary evidence that Levi's friend, Rita Levi Montalcini, a Nobel Prize winner and fellow scientist from Turin, cited immediately as a reason why she judged Levi's death accidental. In fact, when visiting Levi in Turin, I, too, distinctly remember being alarmed by the low inner railing and the worn marble stairs, and hugging the outer wall of the stairwell as a consequence.[8]

Each year, Samuel recounts, April 11 recurs as a double anniversary for him: the anniversary of his liberation from Buchenwald—"my second birth"—and the anniversary of the death of his dear friend. "The spring and summer of 1987," he writes, "was one of the most terrible—the most terrible—of all those that I lived since my liberation." Magavern writes that Levi possessed "a sense of the sacredness of human relations, especially friendship." Samuel's sad and moving memoir is a testament to a sacred bond forged with Levi in an unholy place.

The other standout exemplum in *If This Is a Man* is Henri, the silver-tongued manipulator from the chapter "The Drowned and the Saved." If Jean Samuel is Levi's meritorious alter ego—kind, generous, modest, companionable, capable, loyal (and Null Achtzen is a hated "potential version of himself" as a *Musulman*, a "drowned man"), then Henri represents something else altogether. He is the topsy-turvy alter ego, what Levi once termed an "almost-me, another myself, turned upside down."[9] Henri is the specter of the man that Levi had the potential to become, and most feared becoming. His fear is palpable in his scathing portrait. Indeed, of all the *Häftlinge* in *If This Is a Man*, Henri elicits Levi's greatest scorn.

Fifty years after Levi first portrayed him, "Henri"—Paul Steinberg—published a book of his own, one whose absent interlocutor is unmistakably Primo Levi. Steinberg takes up the threads of the conversation Levi initiated in *If This Is a Man* and offers both his defense and his acquiescence to the charges his former campmate leveled against him. Without self-pity— how ironic for a man accused of using pity as his currency!— and in stark, unapologetic prose, Steinberg's *Speak, You Also* (the 2000 translation of his 1996 *Chronique d'ailleurs*) responds to Levi's wish "to know [Henri's] life as a free man."[10] What emerges, however, are few details of Steinberg's post-Auschwitz life. The ordinary details of a man's existence, like his marriage and children, profession, hobbies, accomplishments and setbacks, are absent. Instead, Steinberg focuses nearly exclusively on his years in the *Lager*, his behavior there, and his judgment of his behavior.

Levi wrote in *The Drowned and the Saved* that there are two kinds of Holocaust survivors: those who talk about the Holocaust incessantly and those who do not talk about it at all. Levi clearly fell into the first category; Steinberg just as clearly fell into the second—until the day he began writing this book. At no time after Auschwitz did he speak of his camp experiences, whether to his family or to his friends. He kept his silence even after reading Levi's accusations and during the explosion of trials and testimony, films, miniseries and books, and Holocaust-linked deaths in the 1980s and 1990s. He picked up the pen only after Levi's death, as "a strange vacation assignment, one I've been planning for fifty years," to be accomplished between retirement and decrepitude.

Levi made something of a straw man out of Steinberg when he recast him as Henri. Steinberg, in Auschwitz, was only 16 years old, though Levi wrote the part of Henri for a 22-year-old—closer in age to Levi's own 24–25 years (there is a vast difference in our world, but especially in the *univers concentrationnaire*, between an adolescent and a young adult). Levi and Steinberg spent a similar amount of time in the camp (11 versus 15 months). Both were slight men and intellectually inclined, and both were Western Europeans in a sea of Ashkenazim. They were both assigned to the Chemical *Kommando* and even had closely-linked tattoos, only 339 digits apart.

Henri is Levi's unbidden doppelganger. With these similarities, both real and invented, Levi brought Henri up close only to dismiss him with seething ferocity. Steinberg's dogged pursuit of survival without recourse to morals repelled and horrified the Italian author. Steinberg, however,

determined that he had to jettison dignity and economize
on emotions in favor of survival by adaptation. As a fresh-
faced teenager, he was aware that he was in great danger,
that he was "fresh meat," and that many of his campmates
were genuinely crazy. Cold calculation set in: in any herd,
he concluded, "the herdsman always has his favorite." After
a year's time, Steinberg congratulated himself. "Sometimes
I think I could have had great expectations for my camp
career if only the experiment had lasted longer."[11] Steinberg's
very being threatened Levi with his willing embrace of moral
vacuity in exchange for raw survival. To deny Henri is to
keep the black holes at bay.

If Levi did not want to have anything to do with Steinberg
post-Lager, it is because he feared seeing his own reflection
in Henri's face. And yet, perhaps if they had met, the accused
could have "persuaded [Levi] to change his verdict by showing
that there were extenuating circumstances." Post-Auschwitz,
Steinberg "lived in humiliation," affectless, pitiless, unmoved
by compassion, a "fireproof and unsinkable being." Was he,
however, a "man" in Levi's terms? Steinberg craved exculpation
from his peer. His book, he insisted, had cleared the "docket";
his "alibi" had been proffered. Levi, who, in "The Gray Zone,"
admitted to a sense of *impotentia judicandi* vis-à-vis many
Auschwitz offenders, was cast as judge and jury by his chagrined former campmate. Steinberg is rueful that he'll never
know whether he had the right to ask clemency. "Can one be
so guilty," he asks, "for having survived?"

Jean Samuel, Charles Conreau, Alberto Dalla Volta: these are
"men" for Levi. He recognizes their worth in those unspeak-
able surroundings and, in the first two cases, in the world

outside the *univers concentrationnaire*. Levi immortalized them and, listening to interviews with the two Frenchmen, it is clear that they idolized him. Samuel's indelible memory of those days became a tribute to his Auschwitz friend in *Il m'appellait Pikolo*. Steinberg, too, cast Levi as his fixed interlocutor in his "chronicle of elsewhere." The "strangest thing," he says, is that he does not remember Levi from Auschwitz at all. Perhaps Levi was not useful to him—but then that might just confirm Levi's judgment.

Primo Levi's Universe allows us to appreciate how Primo Levi became Primo Levi. Magavern speaks to us in an unobtrusive voice and with just enough of an outsider's perspective to leaven the common impulse to hagiography and deliver an exercise in biography. His probing yet restrained stance makes this reader envision an English version of the *torinesità* or true Turinese character that was occasionally ascribed to Levi: reserve, decency, *reticentia*.

When Primo Levi captured my attention in the early 1980s, I wished him to become one of the greats of the twentieth century. Two decades later, I am gratified yet astounded that he has inspired four compelling biographies, scores of articles, dozens of books and numerous conferences. Myriad operas, choreographies, films, and symphonies have been inspired by him and dedicated to him. Rock groups have taken his name, and visual artists have reproduced and reinterpreted his likeness. Levi has become a reference point for study and reflection on Holocaust memory, witness, communication, work, shame, judgment and justice, violence (including "useless violence"), solidarity, moral, political and ideological systems, faith and belief, and others. So fearful of the "shipwreck of reason," Levi instead continues to lead us in the "quiet study of certain aspects of the human mind."[12]

—*Risa Sodi*

NOTES

ABBREVIATIONS USED IN THE NOTES

Black	*The Black Hole of Auschwitz*
Conversations	*Conversations with Primo Levi*
Double	*The Double Bond*
Drowned	*The Drowned and the Saved*
If Not	*If Not Now, When?*
Inferno	*The Divine Comedy, Vol. 1: the Inferno*
Survival	*Survival in Auschwitz*
Mirror	*The Mirror Maker*
Moments	*Moments of Reprieve*
Odyssey	*The Odyssey*
Other	*Other People's Trades*
Periodic	*The Periodic Table*
Poems	*Collected Poems*
Primo	*Primo Levi: a Life*
Reawakening	*The Reawakening*
Search	*The Search for Roots*
Sixth	*The Sixth Day and Other Tales*

Tragedy	*Primo Levi: Tragedy of an Optimist*
Tranquil	*A Tranquil Star*
Voice	*The Voice of Memory: Interviews 1961–1987*
Wrench	*The Monkey's Wrench*

ONE   A NEW COSMOS

1. *Reawakening*, 38. *The Truce* was published in the United States as *The Reawakening*.
2. *Wrench*, 52.
3. *Survival*, 36.
4. *Primo*, 30.

TWO   FROGS ON THE MOON

1. *Primo*, 23; *Double*, 62.
2. *Primo*, 8, 12.
3. Ibid., 21.
4. *Double*, 55.
5. Ibid., 55.
6. *Conversations*, 6.
7. *Primo*, 80.
8. *Other*, 50.
9. Ibid., 53.
10. Ibid., 54.
11. *Primo*, 41.
12. *Other*, 63.
13. Ibid., 65.
14. Ibid., 69.
15. Ibid., 68.
16. *Periodic*, 22.
17. Ibid., 22.
18. Ibid., 24.
19. Ibid., 24.
20. *Voice*, 16.
21. *Primo*, 55.
22. *Tranquil*, 103.

23. *Primo*, 67.
24. *Tranquil*, 104.

Three Black Stars

1. *Periodic*, 23.
2. *Voice*, 175.
3. Ibid., 8.
4. *Periodic*, 52.
5. *Voice*, 61.
6. *Periodic*, 23.
7. Ibid., 41.
8. Ibid., 41–42.
9. Ibid., 53.
10. Ibid., 56.
11. *Search*, 214.
12. Ibid., 214.
13. *Other*, 22–23.
14. Ibid., 23.
15. *Poems*, 29.
16. *Periodic*, 31.
17. Ibid., 31.
18. Ibid., 39.
19. *Primo*, 93.
20. Ibid., 95.
21. Ibid., 94.
22. *Periodic*, 40.
23. Ibid., 42–43.
24. Ibid., 39.
25. Ibid., 48.
26. Ibid., 35.
27. *Double*, 125.
28. Ibid., 126.
29. *Primo*, 92; *Tragedy*, 39.
30. *Double*, 126.
31. *Sixth*, 103.
32. *Double*, 41 (Angier translation).

33. *Other*, 157.
34. *Voice*, 275.
35. *Poems*, 26.
36. *Double*, 80.
37. *Voice*, 92.

FOUR   MAGIC MOUNTAINS

1. *Primo*, 109.
2. *Voice*, 61.
3. *Periodic*, 75.
4. Ibid., 33; *Voice*, 89.
5. *Periodic*, 64.
6. Ibid., 73.
7. *Double*, xvii.
8. Ibid., 216.
9. *Periodic*, 121.
10. Ibid., 118.
11. *Primo*, 120.
12. *Poems*, 3.
13. *Primo*, 139.
14. *Periodic*, 131.
15. *Double*, 474.
16. Ibid., 281–282.
17. *Survival*, 12.
18. *Primo*, 162–166; *Double*, 474.
19. *Reawakening*, 20.

FIVE   HELL'S CIRCLES

1. *Survival*, 23.
2. *Tragedy*, 206.
3. *Survival*, 118.
4. Ibid., 29.
5. Ibid., 89.
6. *Primo*, 258.
7. *Survival*, 9.

8. Ibid., 31, 37.
9. Ibid., 107.
10. *Moments*, 45.
11. *Survival*, 22.
12. Ibid., 112.
13. Ibid., 113.
14. *Moments*, 67; *Drowned*, 38; *Moments*, 57.
15. *Moments*, 51.
16. Ibid., 99.
17. *Drowned*, 16–17.
18. Ibid., 23.
19. *Moments*, 88.
20. Ibid., 170.
21. *Survival*, 5.
22. Ibid., 25.
23. Ibid., 96.
24. Ibid., 96.
25. Ibid., 98.
26. *Black*, 84.
27. Ibid., 6.
28. *If Not*, 109–110.
29. *Drowned*, 202.
30. *Reawakening*, 213 (in the United States, the afterword was published in *The Reawakening*).
31. *Tragedy*, 188.
32. *Poems*, 24.
33. *Drowned*, 16.
34. *Primo*, 293.
35. *Moments*, 92.
36. *Primo*, 323.
37. Ibid., 405.
38. *Moments*, 100.
39. Ibid., 101.
40. Ibid., 101.
41. Ibid., 105.
42. *Moments*, 99–100.
43. *Primo*, 322.

44. *Double*, 582; *Primo*, 326.
45. *Periodic*, 215.
46. *Primo*, 378.
47. *Periodic*, 221–222.
48. Ibid., 221.
49. Ibid., 222.
50. *If Not*, 127.
51. *Survival*, 82.
52. Ibid., 82.
53. Ibid., 8.
54. Ibid., 8.
55. *Black*, 4.
56. Ibid., 17.
57. Ibid., 119.
58. *Primo*, 80.
59. *Survival*, 43.
60. *Voice*, 228–229.
61. *Survival*, 42, 95.
62. Ibid., 88.
63. Ibid., 52.
64. Ibid., 61.
65. *Primo*, 187.
66. *Survival*, 81.
67. Ibid., 79.
68. Ibid., 79.
69. Ibid., 68–69.
70. Ibid., 37–38.
71. Ibid., 38.
72. Ibid., 38.
73. *Tragedy*, 124.
74. Ibid., 142.
75. *Conversations*, 23.
76. *Double*, 289.
77. *Survival*, 94.
78. Ibid., 122.
79. Ibid., 122.
80. *Moments*, 17.
81. Ibid., 18.

82. *Survival*, 37.
83. *Conversations*, 21–22.
84. *Survival*, 145.
85. *Moments*, 52.
86. *Survival*, 84.
87. Ibid., 87.
88. Ibid., 87–88.
89. Ibid., 91.
90. *Drowned*, 82.
91. *Periodic*, 140.
92. *Survival*, 53.
93. Ibid., 83.
94. *Black*, 36.
95. *Drowned*, 43.
96. *Conversations*, 20–21.
97. *Moments*, 10.
98. Ibid., 10.
99. Ibid., 33.
100. Ibid., 167.
101. *Drowned*, 69.
102. *Survival*, 39.
103. *Drowned*, 44.
104. Ibid., 60.
105. Ibid., 40.
106. *Survival*, 35.
107. Ibid., 36.
108. Ibid., 36.
109. *Drowned*, 146.
110. *Moments*, 155.
111. Ibid., 51.
112. Ibid., 51, 53.
113. *Survival*, 118.
114. *Voice*, 275.
115. *Conversations*, 68.
116. Ibid., 67.
117. *Primo*, 105.
118. *Moments*, 112.
119. *Survival*, 51.

120. Ibid., 51.
121. *Tragedy*, 162; *Drowned*, 81.
122. *Voice*, 39.
123. *Moments*, 67.
124. *Survival*, 131.
125. Ibid., 135.
126. Ibid., 156.
127. Ibid., 155.
128. Ibid., 156.
129. Ibid., 156.
130. *Moments*, 10.
131. *Voice*, 223.
132. *Survival*, 84.
133. Ibid., 108.
134. *Double*, 321.
135. *Survival*, 111.
136. Ibid., 111.
137. Ibid., 109.
138. *Survival*, 90, 91, 97; *Primo*, 304.
139. *Moments*, 159.
140. *Periodic*, 44.
141. *Moments*, 158–159.
142. Ibid., 159.
143. Ibid., 160.
144. Ibid., 160.
145. *Survival*, 97.
146. Ibid., 96, 97.
147. Ibid., 101.
148. *Inferno*, 309.
149. *Survival*, 103.
150. Ibid., 104.
151. Ibid., 104–105.
152. *Inferno*, 308.
153. Ibid., 309.
154. *Survival*, 99.
155. *Tragedy*, 176.
156. *Moments*, 11.
157. *Voice*, 17.

158. *Drowned*, 139.
159. *Survival*, 122.
160. Ibid., 122.
161. *Primo*, 202.
162. *Survival*, 143.
163. *Voice*, 7.
164. Ibid., 17.
165. *Survival*, 146.
166. *Wrench*, 52.
167. *Drowned*, 149.
168. Ibid., 150.
169. *Survival*, 59.
170. *If Not*, 185.
171. *Reawakening*, 38.
172. Ibid., 38.
173. *Drowned*, 145.
174. Ibid., 174.
175. *Black*, 24.
176. *Survival*, 128.
177. *Moments*, 10.
178. *Drowned*, 141.
179. *Mirror*, 99.
180. *Tragedy*, 201.
181. *Primo*, 235, 506.
182. *Primo*, 285; *Voice*, 100, 102.
183. *Drowned*, 23.
184. Ibid., 34.
185. *Odyssey*, 239.
186. *Voice*, 3–4.
187. *Drowned*, 141.
188. *Voice*, 88.
189. *Drowned*, 167.
190. Ibid., 167.

Six Truces

1. *Survival*, 9.
2. *Primo*, 214–215.

3. *Reawakening*, 27.

4. Ibid., 25–26.

5. Ibid., 22.

6. *Primo*, 160.

7. *Reawakening*, 2.

8. Ibid., 8.

9. Ibid., 8.

10. Ibid., 45.

11. Ibid., 46.

12. Ibid., 160.

13. Ibid., 141.

14. *If Not*, 324.

15. *Reawakening*, 74.

16. *Search*, 77.

17. *Other*, 136.

18. *Primo*, 60.

19. *Reawakening*, 17.

20. Ibid., 16, 17.

21. Ibid., 18.

22. Ibid., 18.

23. Ibid., 132.

24. Ibid., 132.

25. Ibid., 134.

26. Ibid., 134.

27. Ibid., 66.

28. Ibid., 66.

29. Ibid., 116.

30. Ibid., 66.

31. Ibid., 66.

32. Ibid., 64.

33. Ibid., 117.

34. *Periodic*, 121.

35. *Survival*, 72.

36. *Reawakening*, 28.

37. Ibid., 32, 39.

38. Ibid., 29.

39. Ibid., 39.

40. Ibid., 38.
41. Ibid., 40, 110.
42. Ibid., 65–66.
43. Ibid., 181.
44. Ibid., 185.
45. Ibid., 185.
46. Ibid., 192.
47. Ibid., 193–194.
48. Ibid., 192.
49. *Drowned*, 85.
50. Ibid., 86.
51. Ibid., 86.
52. *Moments*, 172.
53. *Reawakening*, 187–188.
54. *Black*, 137.
55. Ibid., 138–139.
56. Ibid., 137.
57. *Moments*, 167.

SEVEN   LIFE INSIDE THE LAW

1. *Moments*, 11.
2. *Voice*, 162.
3. *Double*, 475.
4. *Periodic*, 126.
5. *Double*, 453–454.
6. *Periodic*, 153.
7. *Conversations*, 66–67.
8. *Periodic*, 153.
9. *Poems*, 7.
10. Ibid., 16.
11. Ibid., 19.
12. *Periodic*, 75.
13. Ibid., 183.
14. *Voice*, 163.
15. *Primo*, 387.
16. Ibid., 367.

17. Ibid., 257.
18. Ibid., 363.
19. *Primo*, 392.
20. *Voice*, 18.
21. Ibid., 18–19.
22. *Periodic*, 199.
23. Ibid., 210.
24. Ibid., 203.
25. *Voice*, 93.
26. Ibid., 95.
27. Ibid., 89.
28. Ibid., 16.
29. *Sixth*, 128.
30. *Voice*, 123.
31. *Wrench*, 79-80.
32. *Other*, 11.
33. Ibid., 11.
34. *Double*, 477.
35. Ibid., 477.
36. Ibid., 564–565.
37. Ibid., 652.
38. *Poems*, 42.
39. *Double*, 602.
40. Ibid., 669.
41. *Primo*, 454.
42. *Double*, 526.
43. *Primo*, 479.
44. *Drowned*, 20–21.
45. *Drowned*, 40; *Survival*, 49.
46. *Other*, 15.
47. *Voice*, 140.
48. Ibid., 19.
49. *Drowned*, 71.
50. *Primo*, 352.
51. Ibid., 309.
52. Ibid., 351.
53. Ibid., 355.
54. Ibid., 442.

55. Ibid., 526.
56. *Voice*, 17.
57. Ibid., 101.
58. Ibid., 14.

Eight Uncertain Hours

1. *Survival*, 6.
2. *Moments*, 11.
3. *Double*, 390.
4. Ibid., 142.
5. Ibid., 207.
6. *Moments*, 10.
7. Ibid., 11.
8. *Survival*, 42.
9. *Double*, 504–505.
10. *Moments*, 11.
11. *Drowned*, 24.
12. *Periodic*, 49.
13. *Survival*, 6.
14. *Conversations*, 43.
15. *Survival*, 6.
16. *Conversations*, 42.
17. *Periodic*, 59.
18. *Voice*, 156.
19. Ibid., 157.
20. Ibid., 158.
21. Ibid., 158.
22. Ibid., 160.
23. *Mirror*, 106.
24. Ibid., 107.
25. *Black*, 140.
26. *Mirror*, 109.
27. *Primo*, 457.
28. *Voice*, 132–133.
29. *Tranquil*, 90.
30. *Double*, 632.
31. *Periodic*, 41.

32. Ibid., 52.
33. *Other*, 172–173.
34. Ibid., 172.
35. Ibid., 171–172.
36. Ibid., 173.
37. Ibid., 173.
38. Ibid., 173.
39. Ibid., 173–174.
40. *Mirror*, 110.
41. *Other*, 170.
42. *Wrench*, 52.
43. *Other*, 132.
44. Ibid., 173.
45. *Voice*, 113.
46. Ibid., 21.
47. *Search*, 5.
48. Ibid., 5.
49. *Periodic*, 151.
50. *Black*, 105.
51. *Periodic*, 153.
52. *Search*, 77.
53. *Conversations*, 47.
54. *Poems*, 56.
55. *Survival*, 54.
56. *Black*, 101.
57. *Double*, 72.
58. *Periodic*, 232.
59. Ibid., 57–58.

NINE   THE THAW

1. *Periodic*, 34.
2. *Sixth*, 93.
3. *Black*, 143.
4. *Mirror*, 9–10.
5. *Double*, 652.
6. *Other*, 159.
7. Ibid., 173.

8. Ibid., 25.
9. Ibid., 28.
10. Ibid., 29.
11. Ibid., 17.
12. Ibid., 17.
13. Ibid., 19.
14. *Poems*, 47.
15. *Double*, 593.
16. *Sixth*, 39.
17. Ibid., 49.
18. *Other*, 102.
19. Ibid., 106.
20. *Sixth*, 213.
21. *Poems*, 39.
22. *Periodic*, 22.

TEN INTO THE SEA

1. *Survival*, 145; for translation as "third" or "fourth" floor, see *Primo*, 531.
2. *Double*, 655.
3. Ibid., 701–702.
4. Ibid., 639.
5. *Poems*, 8.
6. Ibid., 22.
7. *Sixth*, 129.
8. Ibid., 131.
9. *Survival*, 119–120.
10. Ibid., 130.
11. *Drowned*, 76.
12. *Poems*, 33.
13. *Survival*, 102, 103.
14. *Poems*, 33.

ELEVEN WHAT WE MAKE OF EACH OTHER

1. *Voice*, 174.
2. *Other*, 106.

3. *Search*, 178.
4. *Reawakening*, 215.
5. *Other*, 203–204.
6. *Wrench*, 35.
7. *Periodic*, 68.
8. *Drowned*, 89.
9. *Survival*, 14.
10. *Conversations*, 40.
11. *Survival*, 156.
12. *Drowned*, 200.
13. *Black*, 96.
14. *Survival*, 11.
15. Ibid., 103.
16. *Tragedy*, 329.
17. *Voice*, 38; *Primo*, 483.
18. *Voice*, 91.
19. *Conversations*, 66.
20. *Black*, 48.
21. *Sixth*, 160.
22. *Mirror*, 5–6.
23. *Voice*, 37.
24. Ibid., 239.
25. *Black*, 7.
26. *Voice*, 230.
27. Ibid., 220.
28. Ibid., 142, 214.
29. *Tragedy*, 121.
30. *Reawakening*, 12.
31. *Moments*, 10.
32. *Drowned*, 137.
33. *Reawakening*, 196.
34. *Voice*, 41.
35. *Survival*, 22.
36. *Search*, 11.
37. *Drowned*, 36.
38. *Tranquil*, 41.
39. *Sixth*, 13.

40. Ibid., 13.
41. *Search*, 214–215.
42. *Voice*, 92.
43. *Double*, 419, 420.
44. *Voice*, 130.

Afterword

1. This quote and those that follow from my interview with Levi come from "A Last Talk with Primo Levi," *Present Tense* (May/June 1988), reprinted in *Jewish Profiles: The Best of Present Tense* (New York: Jacob Aronson, Inc., 1992) and "An Interview with Primo Levi," *Partisan Review* (1987, Vol. LIV, No. 3).
2. Magavern, 174–175.
3. Magavern, 76. Contrast this with the story of the *Musulman*, Null Achtzen. This strange name—really a number, 018—is comprised of the first three numbers of that particular inmate's tattoo. The number becomes the name by which he is known. Numerologically, "Null Achtzen" corresponds to 0 + 18, where zero equals "null" and 18 corresponds to the Hebrew letters Het and Yod. Het and Yod together form the Hebrew word *chai*, which is closely linked to the noun *chaim*, or life. Therefore, the name/number Null Achtzen literally means "no life"—a perfect designation for a *Musulman*. It will be left for a different setting to discuss whether this utterly suitable name correlates to the facts or to Magavern's postulation of "storytelling" in Levi's narrative (see below).
4. Jean Samuel and Jean-Marc Dreyfus, *Il m'appellait Pikolo: Un compagnon de Primo Levi raconte* (Paris: Robert Laffont, 2007), 94–95 (translation mine). The 2008 Italian translation by Claudia Lionetti is titled *Mi chiamava Pikolo* (Frassinelli: Milan).
5. Ibid, 37. Indeed, Levi writes, "One must realize that the post of Pikolo represented a quite high rank in the hierarchy of the Prominents…" (*If This Is a Man*, 109).
6. Primo Levi, *If This Is a Man* and *The Reawakening* (New York: Summit Books, 1985), 108.
7. Samuel, *op. cit*, 50–51.

8. See also "Primo Levi's Message" in Levi-Montalcini's 1988 memoir, *In Praise of Imperfection: My Life and Work*, trans. Luigi Attardi (New York: Basic Books).

9. Primo Levi, *Moments of Reprieve* (New York: Summit Books, 1986), 100.

10. Paul Steinberg, *Speak, You Also*, trans. Linda Coverdate (New York: Metropolitan Books, 2000). Steinberg admits to *Lager* intrigues, to being obsessed with staying alive, and to being "ferociously determined to do anything to live, ready to use all means at hand, including a gift for inspiring sympathy and pity."

11. Steinberg's language echoes Levi's: "We would also like to consider that the Lager was pre-eminently a gigantic biological and social experiment" (*If This Is a Man*, 87).

12. Marco Belpoliti and Robert Gordon, eds., *The Voice of Memory: Interviews 1961–1987* (New York: The New York Press, 2001), 92; *If This Is a Man*, 9.

SOURCES

WORKS BY PRIMO LEVI
(IN ORDER OF PUBLICATION)

If This is a Man. Published in the United States as *Survival in Auschwitz*. New York: Collier, 1961.

The Truce. Published in the United States as *The Reawakening*. New York: Collier, 1965.

The Periodic Table. New York: Schocken, 1984.

If Not Now, When? New York: Penguin, 1986.

The Monkey's Wrench. New York: Penguin, 1987.

Moments of Reprieve. New York: Penguin, 1987.

Collected Poems. London: Faber and Faber, 1988.

Other People's Trades. New York: Summit, 1989.

The Drowned and the Saved. New York: Vintage, 1989.

The Mirror Maker. New York: Schocken, 1990.

The Sixth Day and Other Tales. New York: Summit, 1990.

The Search for Roots. Chicago: Ivan Dee, 2002.

The Black Hole of Auschwitz. Cambridge: Polity, 2005.

A Tranquil Star. New York: W. W. Norton, 2007.

INTERVIEWS

Belpoliti, Marco and Robert Gordon, eds. *The Voice of Memory: Interviews 1961–1987.* New York: The New Press, 2001.

Camon, Ferdinando. *Conversations with Primo Levi.* Marlboro: Marlboro Press, 1989.

Levi, Primo and Tuilo Regge. *Dialogo.* Princeton: Princeton University Press, 1989.

BIOGRAPHIES

Angier, Carol. *The Double Bond.* New York: Farrar, Straus, and Giroux, 2002.

Anissimov, Myriam. *Primo Levi: Tragedy of an Optimist.* Woodstock: Overlook, 1999.

Thomson, Ian. *Primo Levi: a Life.* New York: Picador, 2002.

OTHER WORKS

Alighieri, Dante. *The Divine Comedy, Vol. I: The Inferno.* New York: Penguin, 1984.

Homer. *The Odyssey.* New York: Anchor, 1963.

INDEX